MW01109491

Today's Prayer and Meditation

Today's Prayer and Meditation

By
Phillip C. Reinke

Strategic Book Publishing and Rights Co.

Copyright © 2017 Phillip C. Reinke. All rights reserved.

No part of this book may be reproduced or transmitted in any form or by any means, graphic, electronic, or mechanical, including photocopying, recording, taping, or by any information storage retrieval system, without the permission, in writing, of the publisher. For more information, send an email to support@sbpra.net, Attention Subsidiary Rights Department.

Strategic Book Publishing and Rights Co., LLC
USA | Singapore
www.sbpra.com

For information about special discounts for bulk purchases please contact Strategic Book Publishing and Rights Co. Special Sales at bookorder@sbpra.net.

ISBN: 978-1-68181-895-5

Dedication

It is better to light a small candle and pray
than to cast a spotlight on your situation for everyone to see.

To Mom, who inspired my writing of this book

To Peggy, a faithful prayer partner

and

To all daily Prayer Warriors

Introduction

Prayer is one of the greatest gifts bestowed upon man. It is a balm that soothes the deepest hurts and a light in the darkest of times. Prayer is a song that sings in times of highest elation and expresses thanksgiving and gratitude in times of humble appreciation.

Prayers are spoken in desperate times. Some prayers are spoken loudly. Other prayers are said silently. There are short prayers and long prayers. There are prayers that are structured and those that are totally ad lib. Trying to capture and categorize the entire spectrum of prayer is impossible.

Prayer has existed throughout all human experience. Many have tried to create a structure for prayer and have failed. In the end, one realizes that prayer springs from one's heart, mind, and body. It flows from a unity of one's being and expresses that unity to a higher consciousness. Prayer is most often needed when one does not have the time or energy to pray.

Today's Prayer and Meditation is for those times when it is difficult to pray, for those seeking inspiration, and for others who just want a prayer. It is a compilation of 365 prayers that can be used daily across an entire year. It is not organized into specific categories but instead assembled in faith. It is my prayer that the path from Day 1 to Day 365 will touch those who are looking for a prayer at the right time, with the right words.

God bless you as you read through the prayers. Remember that before you pray, He knows your needs and He listens.

Starting the Prayer Journey

Prayers can be long or short. The first prayers in this compilation of a year of daily prayers are longer than the later ones. Each prayer is as much a meditation as it is communication with God. Every morning before I do anything else, I ask, "What would You like me to pray about?" I would then pray.

For many years I shared those prayers with close friends, family, and those who asked via text messages. A few years ago I was moved to share the daily prayers on a blog, then with a website, and finally on a Facebook community page. Each day a prayer, a meditation, and a devotion are added to the pages. These sites have documented my prayer journey and will continue to do so. I invite you to join us on the Facebook page "Today's Prayer and Meditation" or on our website, www.todaysprayerandmeditation.com.

We walk through life alone, but we pray together. Prayers in their initial stage may address questions and establish a foundation upon which the future prayer life is built. The prayers at the beginning of this journey do the same. Later on, the prayers focus on specific issues common in people's lives. Some of the prayers address similar topics from a different perspective. It's not about the specific words; it's about the prayer.

It is said that tomorrow is created as a result of today's decisions and by contemplating, through prayer works, to combine one's physical, spiritual, and mental aspects into a powerful triad. Early on, I called prayer communication with God. As important as it is for one to take time to pray and talk to God, it is just as important to listen.

God bless your prayer journey.

Day 1

Today's prayer: Lord . . .

We seek happiness and security and fulfillment, yet all of these desires seem so fleeting. And when we don't get what we want, we fall prey to anger, stress, and depression.

How childish and selfish to do this when things do not happen the way we want. It is then and only then that we finally ask, "Why?"

We do not realize that the answer is clear when we ourselves answer the question "Who are you working for—yourself or God?"

Let us remember that we work for a reason: that reason is always "to be paid for our labor." When we are working for You, we receive the good fruits of labor, and we are paid just what we need. When we work for anyone or anything else, the payment may not be what we wanted—or we may get what we wanted, sadly, with negatives attached.

Herein lies the truth of labor. You have intended our work be fully and completely for You, with every moment by and through Your direction and guidance. Knowing and doing this, we will obtain what we need, rather than what we want, in compensation with those terrible strings attached.

Let what we do bring us satisfaction, happiness, security, and fulfillment because it is done for You. Let us not have to be lowered to the pit of despair to fully realize and act on this simple truth. Help us to see that you get not only *what* you work for but *whom* you work for.

Today we commit our work to You, trusting that we will do the right things at the right time, always in Your name. Keep us ever conscious of the question "Is what we are saying and doing our will in Your name or Your will in Your name?" Isn't it strange how that one simple letter, "y," can make all the difference?

Let us add that one simple letter to our work mission, rather than having to ask why.

Amen.

Day 2

Today's prayer: Lord . . .

We have a saying: "And that's a promise!"

Of all the promises made since the beginning, You have kept every one.

The laws of the universe are absolutely consistent. Every word ever spoken by You has rung true. Thank You for this consistency, for in those promises and the inevitability of them, we can have unwavering faith.

Bring to mind and let us not forget the promise You made to us: "For what I have started in you, I will finish."

This is an amazing thing. We will become what You intended, not in our time but in Yours. Your plan is perfect.

We hear and see only in part, and this often plays into our stress and frustration. Help us to see that we can have Your entire vision for us with this simple recipe: one part Your promise, one part what we see and hear, and a liberal amount of faith.

The picture becomes entirely clear when we see that we are the bread of life and that, like bread, we are instilled with the yeast of faith. Give us this faith, for it causes our life to rise, and we will become just what You promised, as You promised.

Amen.

Day 3

Today's prayer: Lord . . .

As we ponder the universe, we realize that we are no more important than a single grain of sand on a vast beach, and that the true effect we have in this world is no more substantial.

This thought is mind-boggling. It often stops us there without another more important realization: Every grain of sand is on the beach for a purpose. Without each grain fulfilling its purpose, there would be no beach!

Each grain of sand may desire to be a mountain or a boulder, but if that desire were to be granted, the inviting beauty and comfort of the beach would disappear, only to be replaced with a craggy and violent shore.

Help us to see our role in this world with a humble spirit, realizing that we are but grains of sand, yet with the critical value that each grain has. Each of us is but one of billions, of no greater or lesser importance than the others. Let us not desire to be anything other than what we are, for the other desires are futile.

And most of all, help us to see that the grains of sand upon which we walk were once majestic mountains that broke into boulders and, over the course of time, came to their appointed purpose through the elimination of everything that wasn't them.

For it is in this realization that we find the true amazement and wonder of living in this world and that we can change the world, or at least the part that matters, by simply being who we fully are.

Amen.

Day 4

Today's prayer: Lord . . .

We have been told that it is "what's inside that counts."

It doesn't stop there. That is just the beginning. What's inside is the foundation and wellspring from which all great and wonderful things can and do happen.

But what's inside is lifeless unless it becomes "what's outside." Let us not be deceived that it's enough to simply have what's inside. Help us to see that what's inside is ever present in our world today.

And help us to be ever mindful of the fact that what's inside ultimately finds its way out and shows us as we truly are; there is no hiding who we are from ourselves and the world.

Make us aware of who we truly are "inside" so that we can, together, change those things that work quietly and diligently to control us and keep us in our place of mediocrity—and less of who we are meant to be, for who we are ultimately shows in our thoughts, words, and deeds.

"Create in us a clean heart" and help us to see those thoughts, desires, emotions, aspirations, fears, needs, addictions—anything that controls us and binds us from being fully who we are and are meant to be.

Give us the moment-by-moment strength to overcome the challenges and obstacles and grow through internal transformation that is only possible through You and Your loving, gentle kindness.

Amen.

Day 5

Today's prayer: Lord . . .

Let us ever be full of wonder and amazement at the world around us.

Sadly, we are no longer surprised by many of nature's wonders because we are able to predict them before they happen: the exact rising and setting of the sun, the ebb and wane of the tides, the phases of the moon, the locations of the stars and planets in the night sky, and many more. Our knowledge of the order and timing has blinded us from seeing the true majesty of the consistency of the universe.

Today we stand in awe of the creation and all that it holds for us. It truly is a wonder to behold.

We thank You for the absolute consistency that it possesses, because it is through that order and lack of chaos that we can live and can learn of Your plan for us.

The lesson that nature shares through its consistency is that our lives too should function with absolute consistency. As You ordered nature, so order our lives.

Order our lives as You have ordered the universe. In the beginning Your hand took absolute chaos and turned it into this work of wonder, and You looked at it and saw that it was good.

Order our lives. We are part of this universe and not part of the chaos. We are no less than any part of creation—no less than the sun, the moon, the stars—and we look to remove any and all chaos from our lives.

Order our lives and let us stand in awe and wonder at the consistency that they hold for us.

Let today be as it was in the beginning, and as You look upon us, remove all that chaos. Order our lives and see that we are the work of Your hands, and we are good.

Amen.

Day 6

Today's prayer: Lord . . .

The Internet and our social networks are full of pictures that we have taken of ourselves. We call them "selfies."

It has become one of the most prevalent phenomena on the Internet, and experts have found that we are doing this because the virtual world has put physical distance between us.

We have an innate need to let others know we are real. We use selfies to convey our feelings and to send messages to the world at large without having to say a word. Selfies fulfill a basic need that resides in all of us. We are "selfies."

Open our eyes to a deeper understanding of ourselves and allow that insight to bring us closer to You. And open our eyes to a deeper understanding of You that also brings You into our world.

We often feel a vast distance between You and us. We feel detached from Your presence. Have you ever taken a selfie? Amazingly, the answer is yes! You have made an image that we can see at any moment if we just look, for we are made in Your image. We are Your selfie and can bring You into this world in a real way.

We are more than Your feet and hands. We are Your heart and emotions. We see the fulfillment of Your need and our need for You to be ever present in this world.

When we feel that You are distant or when we feel that You do not care, open our minds to Your selfie and let us see that You are truly beside us and inside us, for we are created in Your image and are Your selfie. Let us act that way

Amen.

Day 7

Today's prayer: Lord . . .

Does it really matter?

Our talk is filled with clichés such as "I only get upset by the things that matter, and nothing really matters." You have advised to "put aside the petty and focus on what really matters." As we contemplate our lives in the perspective of the universe, it's all petty. Does anything really matter?

Your advice is perfect, yet we live with anger, hurt, sorrow, fear, insecurity, jealousy, and many other negative and destructive emotions.

Help us to see what our petty feelings are doing to us and those around us, for any negative emotion has a negative outcome and is not truly the fault of the other person. It is most often a personal problem that can be likened to "taking poison and expecting the other person to die."

Make "putting aside" an integral part of our being and of how we live, for every moment lost in ill will is a chance for happiness that, sadly, is lost forever.

Heal the wounds caused by anger, hurt, ego, greed, and entitlement—any and all emotions and thoughts that do not matter. Let us see that these feelings automatically open the door to loss: loss of friends, loss of family, and most of all loss of a chance to live in the abundance of happiness and forgiveness.

We ask again, "Does it matter?" And the answer is it does!

But what matters is not what we think or feel, but what we do! Help us to do it right!

Amen.

Day 8

Today's prayer: Lord . . .

You are the author of our lives. You have not only placed our names in the book of life, You have written our entire life story.

As we ponder our lives, Your attention to every word is amazing. More amazing is Your use of punctuation.

Today we see Your use of the semicolon. Good authors know when to stop writing. They end the sentence and start another.

Great authors always have a little more to say and use the semicolon at the end of the first sentence so that they can add more clarity and refinement, not unlike the way You have written our life stories.

"Be patient; God is not finished with me yet" could never be more true!

Thank You for using the semicolon in our lives, for we seek clarity, definition, and more direction. Like a great writer, You give us just what we need in every chapter of our lives and add the critical clarity at exactly the right time.

At times we may be at a loss for words, other times we say too much, and still others we say the wrong things.

Let us not think that we can write our own story. It is for us to read and live, letting us take full control of every word and, more important, the punctuation.

Let the right sentences of our lives end with a period; let still others end with an exclamation point; let the important ones continue with a semicolon. You are truly not finished with us yet!

Amen.

Day 9

Today's prayer: Lord . . .

Which comes first, the chicken or the egg?

A proverbial question. Many times the answer is "It doesn't matter," and sometimes what comes first makes all the difference!

Throughout our walk in this world, we seek peace of mind, body, and spirit, and to that end we believe that if we can just see and understand the reason, we will find peace.

Which comes first, understanding or peace?

The world would have us believe that understanding and logic lead to peace, and it often temporarily does. However, You told us to pray to receive "the peace that surpasses understanding," and contrary to what the world and our mind want, we should be seeking lasting peace, from which true understanding follows. Amazingly, we will often see that understanding is inconsequential to possessing real peace, especially in matters of faith.

Help us to be constantly seeking peace. When we lack peace, help us to look inward and search our hearts, for peace is not externally dependent but a state of being coming from within. And through that search let us find the reasons for our lack of peace and help us to act such that we "create in us clean hearts." Peace is the fruit of a clean heart. Let that harvest be bountiful, providing thoughts, words, and acts that are good, true, and beautiful.

For when we live our lives as such, peace is nothing more than a by-product of the good that we do.

Help us to make our lives models of peace through reflection on ourselves and cleansing of the source of the discord. Whether or not we understand, we will possess the true, important, and lasting gift of peace.

Amen.

Day 10

Today's prayer: Lord . . .

You once gave a sermon in which the word "consider" was used many times—"consider the lilies"—and we underplay the importance of what You were telling us. To us, "consider" is a soft suggestion that we take as meaning that we can take it or leave it as we see fit. This is the furthest thing from the truth.

The true importance of the word is found at the end of Your sermon: "Do not let your mind be filled with anxiety." The real meaning of the word "consider" is more like "Think about this and completely and fully understand."

What You were saying was not soft; there were no options given. What You were saying was a fact. In a very subtle way You gave us important insight into the role that our mind plays on our journey.

Our mind can be filled with energy, excitement, and faith or it can be filled with fear, anxiety, and doubt—one or the other but never both.

Our mind uses whatever resides in it to convince our heart and guide our decisions and actions.

Help us to empty our minds of anxiety and worries and live as the lilies and the sparrows, filled with excitement, free from fear, lacking doubt, and fully secure in Your promises and guidance. These are the true ingredients in the recipe for faith.

Let our minds be emptied of any negative thoughts and replaced in equal measure with one of those things that free us from the bondage of anxiety and faithless action.

You came to set us free. Let us not stand in the way of freedom, but let us come to You with an open mind that can be properly filled with faith so that our hearts guide us to right action.

Amen.

Day 11

Today's prayer: Lord . . .

How many times have we heard or said, "Been there, done that"?

The past has an interesting way of deceiving us. We often believe that our experience is universal and applicable to others going through similar situations. We believe that through our experience we become wise, giving us the license to judge and guide others.

This is true in part but not universal. We are given the gift of wisdom to guide our own lives, but not the lives of others.

Save us from the trap of "thinking themselves wise, they become but fools."

Wisdom can quickly turn into judgment. We ask that You instill in our hearts that judgment is Yours and Yours alone.

Help us to realize that judgment is more than the determination of the "wrongness" of a thought, act, or situation, but also the "rightness"!

It is just as bad to say something is good for another as it is to say it is bad. Loving guidance has no room for judgment. What we are experiencing is between us and You. What others are experiencing is between them and You. What's good for us may lead to the demise of others.

The truly wise, instead, say that they would or wouldn't do something themselves and leave it at that! It is up to the person to decide for themselves.

It is, then, for us to lovingly support the decision, just as You do with us and for us!

Living decisively is about following our heart with the wisdom imparted through our experience for ourselves—and most important, through the realization that what we have is more than enough to get us through for us and us alone.

Help us to see that if there must be judgment, it is only between ourselves and our actions in relationship to what You have made us to do.

Let us be critical of ourselves and use that judgment wisely.

We ask that, as fire refines rock into gold, reduce us to beings of pure value. Make us into vessels worthy of containing nothing but Your love, acting as You would have us act: in wisdom and in love.

Amen.

Day 12

Today's prayer: Lord . . .

Today we ponder a law of nature: "focus."

We focus light to see clearly and focus it further to cut the strongest of substances.

Light in its normal state is so subdued yet ever present, but when focused contains energy unimaginable, able to convey information and powerful enough that it cannot be resisted.

We ask, "Is the power of light found in the light or is it in the focus?"

The answer is actually both! And this question gets more interesting when we look at ourselves as "Your light" to this world.

Just like light, in our normal state we are present.

Just like light, our impact is often subdued and minuscule.

Just light, when slightly concentrated we are able to carry valuable information with clarity.

Just like light, when we are focused we become unstoppable! We are just like light!

Help us to become the true light to this world as You intended, serving the right purpose at the right time, and let us seek "focus of purpose" so that we are unstoppable—at Your appointed time and according to Your purpose.

Interestingly, we are more than a figurative representation of the light of this world. According to the laws of physics, matter is simply "light slowed down." More mind-blowing is the fact that because we are matter, You have actually made us "living light," capable of following Your direction and guidance.

Let us see that we are more than the traditional and figurative "light of this world." We are the real and living light, capable of using the laws of nature to Your glory and for the benefit of others according to Your perfect plan.

And most of all, we have the ability to be focused and unstoppable.

Amen.

Day 13

Today's prayer: Lord . . .

We have quaint little axioms to guide us in almost every aspect of our lives.

When choosing a diamond we have the "4 Cs": color, clarity, cut, and carat.

Not unlike us, each diamond is unique. Not unlike us, each diamond begins as a rough stone of little or no value until the hand of a jeweler carves away the rough edges and shapes it to its intended purpose and then polishes the remaining surfaces, allowing light to reflect, refract, and pass straight through.

We are Your diamonds, chosen while we were but a rough stone. We have but one purpose; we have but one "cut." Make us a "cut above the rest." Remove everything from our lives that separates us from the shape of our purpose.

All diamonds have imperfections. In most cases they are inconsequential. When they are numerous, the diamond's value decreases. We too have imperfections. Unlike with a diamond, our flaws can be removed. Work within us to create perfect clarity so that there is nothing in our lives that impairs our service and purpose.

Color is important to a diamond and is the result of minute traces of other elements being present. Color makes each diamond unique and special. We too are unique and special because of the minute traces of the experiences and knowledge that color our lives. The color of a diamond is set at the moment if creation, as is ours. But You have the ability to adjust and alter our color. We ask that You do so, perfectly controlling what is needed to accomplish what we are destined to do.

Some diamonds are big; other diamonds are small. No matter what size each is, they are still diamonds. Some of us are big and are meant to do big things; others are small and meant to do small things. Regardless of our size and purpose, we are still Your diamonds and should never compare our carats to those of others. Each of us is precious in Your sight. We all are diamonds.

When it's all said and done, diamonds are just gemstones. They have no real value. The value that they are given lies within the heart of the owner. Our value comes from You and Your heart. Let us never forget this fact.

Thank You for believing that we are precious, for without You we are as valuable as a simple rock.

Work the 4 Cs into our lives and make us into the perfect diamond of our world. Another saying that we have is that we are "diamonds in the rough." We see that You are not yet done bringing us to perfection.

Amen.

Day 14

Today's prayer: Lord ...

There are days when our plates are full and our cups overflow with things that we believe we have to do. This is both a blessing and a burden.

How do we accomplish all these things?

Help us to constantly remember that we are called to a single purpose, not only in our life as a whole but in every moment.

Multitasking is the great deception of this age. We are truly only capable of doing one thing well at a time. Yet we have so much to do.

Why?

There is always a reason that we are overloaded. It may be that we put off an important activity when we should have done it. Other times we give lesser activities equal importance to important ones. Other times we use some activity to divert us from those activities we need to but don't want to do. We may be too sick or too tired; we may just not want to do it.

Whatever the reason, it's our fault, *not* Yours.

Let us remember that we have but one thing to accomplish so that we can move forward and accomplish another.

A "good and faithful servant" or "Your instrument" cannot pick and choose what he or she does and doesn't do. "Does the clay have the right to tell the potter what to do?"

Clear our minds and hearts of distractions so that we can focus and accomplish our appointed tasks quickly and fully enjoy the fruits of success. We are but clay; shape us with Your loving and gentle hands.

Help us to see that distractions not only slow our pace but also drain the joy of living.

Focusing in the moment distills and concentrates the happiness and provides us with authentic joy that lasts and builds upon the next activity.

Our mind easily falls prey to distractions. Work with us and order our lives. Show each of us how to ignore those distractions and prioritize our lives so that focus, accomplishment, and joy become second nature to us.

And more important, make this the way we constantly live our lives—no matter who we are, no matter what talents and capabilities we possess or lack. Whether we focus or are distracted is our decision. Let us live a life decided, and correctly decided. There is no valid excuse for us to remain distracted from our mission by decisions that have no impact or those that take us in the wrong direction, so take control and focus our lives.

Amen.

Day 15

Today's prayer: Lord . . .

We are constantly torn. We desire to be "new" and grow into "more," yet we also seek stability and security, wanting that to be our "normal" way of living.

Do we have to be constantly at odds with our goals and aspirations, or can we combine them into a single way of living?

We pray that You combine them into one and remove the divisions that keep us from experiencing the fullness of the life we could be living.

Make our lives into a "new normal" and help us so that we live in a way that takes us higher and higher, making us closer and closer to what we are meant to be.

"A house divided cannot stand." Help us to see that division and conflict open the door to failure, and failure will take every opportunity it is given to enter our lives, whether we are at odds with ourselves or with others.

Create in us hearts that seek the new normal with complete faith, focus, and determination, shielded from the deception and temptations of the world that live around us and within us.

You promised that we would become new creatures. Let that transformation begin today and carry forward every day that remains in our lives.

Let "normal" not stand in the way of that change, but instead turn the new normal into the vehicle that drives us to all we are meant to be—legends in our own right, which is right only when driven in faith and according to Your call.

Amen.

Day 16

Today's prayer: Lord . . .

Help us always to remember that service is fulfilled through meeting the terms of the recipient, regardless of what we believe.

Let us never be deceived into believing that success is on our terms and that we define success!

We rightly believe that we will be happy, content, and secure when we are fulfilling our purpose, but we often forget that our purpose is to be "beings of service" and that we will never achieve success and its fruits on our terms. Sadly, living on our terms will often stagnate us or take us backward!

What we do and don't do is ultimately our decision, but we need to look to You for more than simple guidance and embrace Your choice for us in faith. What we can do and can't do are the same!

It is also our final decision, but our faith in Your promises is tested in this situation. What we decide matters.

Let us always remember that we will never be given anything that we cannot accomplish. What we can or can't do is, again, Your decision for us to faithfully follow.

Help us to see what lack of faith in that promise will do to us, and remember that what stands in front of us has been chosen by You. Not trying because we lack confidence in our abilities automatically destines us for failure, negating faith!

Help us also to remember: Where there is confidence, faith does not reside. Where there is faith, confidence and ability are unnecessary.

Confidence does nothing but keep us in our place and retard our growth. Often our need for confidence is a deception of our mind. Open our eyes and help us to see when it is an attempt of our mind to keep us in our place and not allow us to live in faith.

Faith is the soil in which the most beautiful seeds of personal growth sprout, grow, blossom, and finally bear fruit, providing the most bountiful and sweetest harvest of true, lasting success and authentic happiness.

Let us increase the size of our garden of faith. Let that garden be completely filled with fertile soil, and let that soil be well tilled, free from the weeds of our past failures and sustained by the warmth of Your love and the life-giving water of faith.

Make us fearless in our pursuit of success and happiness. Let what we do shine like a beacon, drawing others to You and taking their lives to higher levels because they are inspired by the legends that You have created in us!

Amen.

Day 17

Today's prayer: Lord . . .

Help us to ask ourselves, "Are we living lives that will be remembered, and will we be missed?"

What we do lives on in the minds or the hearts of others—one or the other, but not both! Where do we want to live after we are gone: in the minds or hearts of others?

Our lives leave indelible impressions—the good that we do and also the things we do out of selfishness, anger, vindictiveness, spite, fear, guilt, and so on.

The "bad" in our lives may be forgiven, but it is not forgotten. It is simply a cold, hard fact.

Open our eyes and let us see that, at the end of it all, we will either be remembered or we will be missed.

After we are gone, figuratively or literally, the echoes of our acts will resound in either other people's minds or in their hearts. The bad we've done will live in their minds. The things we do will be remembered as cold facts.

The good we've done will live in their hearts and be missed, and it will warm their being every time it comes to light.

What has been done in the past is set. Some will be missed. Some will be remembered and forgiven but not forgotten.

But those facts will not matter if they are overpowered by the acts of love that continue to warm the hearts in which they live.

Let us strive to live so that all we do from today forward will be missed and will be more than a cold fact, but one of warmth, caring, and love.

Make every lasting impression of us live in the hearts of others, for the heart is the sole residence of love, and every action done in love lives there and will be missed.

Let us act not to be coldly remembered as a fact but missed for our warmth and for Your love, which was brought into their lives through our actions.

Amen.

Day 18

Today's prayer: Lord . . .

The power of prayer is found in the word "share."

We ask that today's prayer multiplies tenfold or even a hundredfold, and that You make each of us the reason it grows!

Move us to share today's prayer with ten of our friends and pray that those we share it with do the same. Our prayer is for everyone, and it is meant to go beyond ourselves. Let us not just read this prayer but be moved to share the gift.

Today we pray for prayer.

We pray with and for those who are blessed, grateful, and thanking You for the wonderful blessings that You have given them .

We pray with and for those who are in need of physical healing. Touch them in special ways that only You can.

We pray with and for those who are overcome with sadness, fear, or hurt. Bring them peace of mind and comfort.

We pray with and for those who are repressed and hungry. Feed their hearts and souls and bodies and minds.

We pray with and for those who have needs that we are unaware of. Provide their needs beyond our awareness.

Let the simple fact that we are in prayer, and that others see that we are praying for and with them, be sufficient. Let that sufficiency be in more than just the words we share. Let our lives reflect our prayers.

Make our lives prayers to You and the answers to the prayers reflected in our actions. That is, when we experience the fullness of prayer and authentic happiness, move us to pray and act. This is the greatest gift of prayer, for You know everyone's needs better than we do. It is not that we pray for specifics or use the words that matters; it is the fact that we are united in prayer. Help us to always remember this.

The truth is that we are united in prayer, and because we are united, we share through our actions not just words but Your love for them. It is through our actions that our prayers become real.

Make today's prayer one that changes the world—or at least the part that matters! And the part that matters is how we act.

Make our lives prayers: to You, with You, for You.

Amen.

Day 19

Today's prayer: Lord . . .

How did they know?

"As far as the east is from the west, He separates us from our transgressions."

This line was written thousands of years ago. We read this passage from Psalms and we automatically focus on the message of the totality of forgiveness, and we miss an amazing piece of insight that shows how You worked in the words that we hold dear!

The psalmist could have said as far as north is from south, but as we think about this, we realize a person can travel north and at a certain point they will be heading south, or vice versa when traveling north or south. Its opposite is inevitable.

How did they know that a person can travel east or West forever? As long as we travel east or west, the opposite is only possible if we turn around; otherwise we can travel in that direction forever.

Was this just a good guess?

This passage was written long before we really knew that the earth was round and long before we assigned lines of latitude and longitude, yet those words were written and still hold entirely true.

How did they know?

The answer is simple: They didn't. You did!

These words, like many others spoken by Your children, were not their words but Yours—words inspired, heard, and remembered. Inspired words carry lasting truth and impact because they are Your words.

We pray for and seek Your inspiration. Fill us with Your words. Help us to direct them appropriately so that their impact is as far-reaching into the lives of those for whom they are intended, as the words of the messengers and prophets of the past have been on this world.

Inspiration is not dead. It lives, and we simply need to be receptive to its presence.

Give us the receptiveness and openness to faithfully passing the inspiration on.

People will ask, "How did you know?"

And our answer will be, "We didn't. God did!"

We pray that You make inspiration a regular part of our lives and the answer to that question.

Most of all, let us see beyond the traditional interpretations and open our minds to the deeper meanings of the words already given to us:

"As far as the east is from the west, He separates us from our transgressions."

Seeing that forgiveness creates an infinite distance between us and our transgression, unless we turn around and walk back.

Amen.

Day 20

Today's prayer: Lord . . .

What's left to see?

Because of Your loving forgiveness, You do not see these things in us that we have done that do not follow Your perfect will. Take those things away and what's left to see? This is a question that we need to be asking ourselves moment by moment.

Help us to see ourselves as You see us, and use that image to move us to grow and to serve.

Make our lives such that as You look at our thoughts, You see purity and caring at our feet. You see our feet running to the aid of people in need and filling their hands. Take us to those whose hands are outstretched and begging for handouts and help, as the burdensome individuals who grow fat on the labor of others do, but instead working so that they are never a burden on their friends and families.

In our hearts You see nothing but containers of Your love. Strip away the world from our lives today and give us the passion to live larger than we have ever lived.

What do You see when You look at us? Do You see an individual larger than life? Or do You have to strain to see anything at all?

Let all that we think, say, and do add to our image such that You can see us and declare, "Good job, faithful servant."

Amen.

Day 21

Today's prayer: Lord . . .

We do not fear change. We fear loss!

We ask to become a new creature with trepidation because we have become comfortable with who we are and who we believe we should be.

Make us new creatures, unbounded by our pasts and fully free to be what we were designed to be. Clean our houses, literally and figuratively.

It is only through and by Your grace that we are able to cast off that which stands in the way of fully loving You and serving our purpose.

Make it so that we are no longer overwhelmed by the disarray and confusion of this world. Give us the ability to focus on that which is good, true, and beautiful so that we are truly new creatures. Help us to see what we have to gain by losing who we are.

Amen.

Day 22

Today's prayer: Lord . . .

"All things are possible . . ."

Help us to search our hearts and consider that what we believe may stand in the way of our fully experiencing what You intended for us.

We often do not realize that logic and the search for facts cause us to strip away and reject possibilities.

"Thinking themselves wise, they become but fools."

This exercise of life is important but also limiting.

"When I was child, I believed as a child. When I became an adult, I discarded childish beliefs."

This makes sense to us, yet "unless you become as a child, you cannot enter the kingdom."

Help us to regain and never lose that childlike sense of awe and wonder at the vast possibilities afforded to us in the universe.

Help us to regain the childlike traits that are the key to the kingdom of heaven and to never again lose them.

Open our eyes to the fact that any knowledge we possess is for the moment and the moment only, and that "we see in part," and it is sufficient to get us through.

Also help us never to judge others for their position in life or for their beliefs, but to lovingly accept where they are and guide them into a deeper understanding of themselves and the world around them.

The destination and the purpose of our "journey of growth" are achieved not through limitation but through realization of the breadth and depth of Your presence and love.

The size of Your universe is infinite. It is only made smaller by our rejecting the possibilities it affords. All things are indeed possible. These possibilities live in our hearts and not in our minds, which work to convince us that the limits are truth.

You are the truth. Open our hearts so that we are ruled by You and the limitless possibilities that are around us and so that we again become as children.

Amen.

Day 23

Today's prayer: Lord . . .

What do we *need* to do today? How do we know it's right? We ask this question of ourselves daily—or at least we should!

Some of us are future oriented, working to build a better tomorrow.

Some of us are focused on today, working to ensure the foundation upon which we build a better tomorrow is firm.

Some of us are spontaneous, living moment by moment, ensuring that what is happening now sends something good into tomorrow.

Some of us don't care.

Who's right? What do we need to do?

The answer is quite simple.

The answer is the same for everyone.

Yet that answer is unique for every person in this world. Still, there is a common thread that runs through each answer, by which we can judge the rightness of our actions.

And our purpose—this is what we are obligated to do in every case.

Regardless of our calling, we are charged to leave every moment better for our having been allowed to participate. Participation is a gift, but a gift with a cost!

That cost is gratitude.

Let us not forget the price we are to pay. "This is the day the Lord has made. Let us be glad and rejoice."

Let our gratitude extend beyond words into our every action, for if we are truly thankful, it shows in what we think, say, and do.

Let our thoughts be pure, good, true, and focused.

Let our words be ones of comfort, inspiration, or support— always uplifting and full of hope.

Let our actions never to be a burden to others in the moment because we think our needs are greater than those of the people upon which we depend or ask.

Let us leave every moment better for our having been in it. Moments come and go. Let not one moment be wasted.

What we need to do is what we are doing, for this moment and every one that follows.

Help us leave it better and be driven by gratitude, for each one was made especially for us and is a gift.

Help our thankfulness and gratitude go beyond our words and flavor our every action.

Amen.

Day 24

Today's prayer: Lord . . .

"I go to prepare a place for you."

After hearing these words, why do we worry about the future? Our fears and anxieties are not a matter of fact but stem from a lack of faith. We deeply desire to live peaceful lives, fully secure in how tomorrow will be.

Open our eyes to the fact that what the world offers and wants us to believe is nothing more than a shell game that attempts to distract us from the current fear and momentarily divert our attention so that we are unprepared for what is to come.

Also help us to see that this world offers nothing that will make tomorrow any different or better. It prepares nothing ahead of time for us.

Open our eyes to the fact that tomorrow is prepared for us—it is a promise, Your promise—and that we have no reason to fear. There is no reason for any anxiety. Fear and anxiety are the wrong answer to the test of faith!

Let our lives ace this exam.

Let our faith remove those things that stand in the way of our being able to prepare for tomorrow.

Let all of our actions be perfectly aligned with what we need to do to enhance the preparations that You are making for tomorrow specially for us. When we arrive at tomorrow, it will be what it was meant to be and it will be exactly what we intended, and we will do exactly what we need to do.

With You for us, how can we fail?

This is the confidence that we have in Your promises, and faith in those promises is what will remove fear and anxiety.

We will see You tomorrow, or at least we will see what You have done in preparation for our arrival. Because You have moved on to the next tomorrow to prepare that for us.

Amen.

Day 25

Today's prayer: Lord . . .

It is ironic that the days when we don't have time to pray or don't feel like praying are the days that we need prayer the most.

This is a struggle common to all of us and a battle that we need to overcome to experience the fullness of life in this world.

Help us to make talking *with* You an integral and regular part of our daily routine.

You began teaching this at Your last supper with Your disciples. You suggested that whenever we ate or drank, we should remember You!

How brilliant of You to relate prayer to an essential and regular part of living. We eat often; remembering to pray or actually praying each time we eat or drink ensures that it becomes as much a part of us as the food we eat!

Help us to also see that prayer is true communication, which means that we are not just talking to You but also listening to what You are saying in return.

Help us to hear the words of nature in the wind and rain, the roar of thunder in the silence of warming sunshine.

Help us to hear Your words in the touch of a friend, in their words of comfort, advice, or admonition. Most of all, give us trust through our ever-growing faith in the words that You place in our own hearts.

Let today be the beginning of a new chapter of our lives in which we are no longer distracted from fulfilling our responsibility to pray, for in the end we aspire to "pray without ceasing."

And when we arrive at that place in our lives, we will truly understand what it means to make our lives prayers to You!

Amen.

Day 26

Today's prayer: Lord . . .

It is said that infancy is the most difficult time in our life. It is then that we exist oblivious to the truth around us because we are totally lacking experience and strength. We are totally dependent on others.

Sadly, the same is said in adolescence, although we think differently. Then the teen years, as we strive to prove our independence, then adulthood, when we are constantly confronting an ever-changing world.

It seems like every stage of our life is filled with difficulties and challenges. Help us to see the common message carried by the lesson hidden within every stage of life, which many do not see or understand.

Regardless of what stage in our life we are at, we always lack the experience and strength to meet the real challenges of today and tomorrow. That is what growing is all about!

If we only knew today yesterday, for what we have is hindsight. What we lack is the true present and future sight that You possess. Help us to trust Your view and influence through others.

Help us to be children who look to You and others for the experience and strength needed to be fully successful and authentically happy. When we go it alone, we have nothing but our past to depend upon and we risk failure.

When we look to You and Your guidance, we have all we need and we risk nothing.

Show us what to do. Make our todays and tomorrows complete, for when we know that Your hand is in our lives, our cups will truly run over with Your blessings and touch those nearest us.

Amen.

Day 27

Today's prayer: Lord . . .

How do we know that You are here?

Open our eyes to the fact that it is through us that You enter this world. We are the channels through which Your love and grace are shown and shared . Even a seemingly insignificant interaction holds the potential to be life-changing.

Make us keenly aware of what we say and do, and what we don't say and neglect to do can be life-changing for us and for those we touch.

Temper our speech and actions so that they show only love and caring, for the world is to change because of us.

Let all that we do be focused on the part that matters and let it always be for the best and to Your glory.

Amen.

Day 28

Today's prayer: Lord . . .

Every word . . .

Let every word that emanates from our mouths be uplifting and constantly carrying Your message of understanding and love.

Bring to us a realization that our spoken words are meant to serve and lift others; they are not meant to lift ourselves up at the expense of others.

"Gird" our tongues and make it part of our nature to see the impact of our words.

The world wants us to believe that we need to be assertive and stand up for our rights. You taught us to "turn the other cheek," for You are our protector.

"With You for us, who can be against us?"

Let us remember that gem of wisdom before we speak harshly.

Let us remember that taking any aggressive or assertive role is saying that we can do it better than You.

Let our words be tempered.

Remind our hearts that blunt or brutal honesty is often hurtful and contrary to living with love and gentleness.

Open our eyes to the fact that we are instruments of healing and comfort, not intentional pain.

There is no justification for words not spoken from the heart, not spoken in love, not spoken with the utmost care and compassion.

Anger, frustration, and injustice are not our problem but "their" problem. Move us to prayer in every instance when we are tempted to speak out wrongly.

Remind us of the caring love that You have shown to us and allow that reminder to spark actions of love and forgiveness like the ones You have shown to us.

Let every word that we say or write or share, publicly or privately, be the ones You want us to carry, for we are Your representatives. Because of that, remind us that every word is to be Your words. Do not let what we say or write misrepresent You in any way, shape, or form.

Every word . . .

Amen.

Day 29

Today's prayer: Lord . . .

We have a saying: "You are what you eat." This saying is true in its literal translation. We see the effects that eating healthy has on our body, and it is also true in a deeper, more figurative way!

Help us to see that anything that enters our being ultimately becomes part of us.

Help us to become less tolerant of anything that could separate us from fulfilling our mission.

Help us to see what it means to be "in it but not of it." Our apathy and tolerance go beyond affecting our own being; they license others to continue acting such that they are not leaving the moment better for their participation in it.

We may hear it, but we don't have to listen.

We may see it, but we don't have to watch.

We don't have to judge it as good or bad.

We don't have to take it in because it does not benefit us.

Help us to avoid all manner of things that misrepresent You and Your love and caring, whether it be from outside, taken in, or coming from inside our minds and going outward.

Let all that we "eat," the "food" to each of our senses, benefit our being so that we grow healthy—not only in body, but also in mind and spirit.

And let that same food that we share outwardly do the same for others, bringing them closer to You, and never bringing You shame or pushing others further from You.

Amen.

Day 30

Today's prayer: Lord . . .

What is the secret of living in the peace and security that we long for, free from anxiety and fear?

Some of those who are praying and some for whom we are praying have had restless nights because of those things, and many of those will carry that into their day. Sadly, hunger, loneliness, insecurity, fear, and other negative feelings have become our way of life.

You said those things will always be with us. Show us where comfort is hidden.

You have taught us that regret and guilt are the emotions of the past and that, because of You, there is no need to carry them into the present.

You also taught us that fear, anxiety, and their "cousins" are emotions of the future. We do not have to invite them back into our present.

Knowing these truths may be comforting, but *believing* them is the critical first step in the journey that frees us from their shackles.

Strengthen and amplify the words that You told us, and turn Your words from simple knowledge into a belief. You know, as do we, that we truly only act on what we believe.

This simple change will clear the present of the distractions that diligently work to drain the joy and happiness of the moment and keep us away from You.

And as "one good step leads to another," help us to embrace the gifts that strengthen our day further.

Help us to always remember to close our day with a prayer of gratitude, and wake us with a spirit of anticipation.

These are the fortress walls that will ultimately repel any attack from the things that attempt to hold us at bay.

And during the day, as the attacks grow, let us shore up those walls with more gratitude and anticipation so that our emotional enemies never get in.

Thank You for showing us that the secret to authentic joy and happiness is found by resisting and repelling that which works to destroy us—for, as You said, those things will always be among us.

We believe that by Your grace, and with gratitude and anticipation, we can be unaffected by them. Because of what we believe, we can be "in it but not of it."

Amen.

Day 31

Today's prayer: Lord . . .

How often were we told as children or have we told our own children to focus?

Many of us wrongly believe that we can discard that important guidance when we become adults—or at least we act like it. In actuality it is as true for adults as it is for children. We can only be successful when we focus.

Demands and distractions are a fact of life. Our days are filled with many important demands. They are also filled with demands that we think are important but in truth are not.

This is one of the ways the world effectively keeps us in our place. We ask that You change this attitude in us and help us to grow.

We pray that You "order our days." Help us to see that we can truly do one thing in excellence at a time.

Focus.

Help us to see Your ordering of our lives and to focus in faith, knowing and believing that Your order is perfect and is exactly what we should be doing.

Give us focus and help us to "trust in You with our whole heart."

Keep us from being distracted by the noise of the world around us, which causes us to lose focus and diverts us from the very things that we have been designed to accomplish.

Keep us from "leaning on our understanding," for "we see only in part."

Let us see just how unique we really are, planned before the "beginning of time" for one specific reason or mission, for every moment that we walk this earth.

Through that realization, motivate us to fulfill that mission through our focus on doing in every moment that which You planned—with focus.

When we were children, it was difficult because of all the things we had to learn.

When we were teens, it was hard with all the distractions.

When we are adults, it is hard because of all the things we have to do.

Let us take just a moment and listen.

Let us hear Your living word of guidance.

Focus . . .

Amen.

Day 32

Today's prayer: Lord . . .

"And lean not on your own understanding."

Why? It's an often asked, if not the most often asked, question.

We are constantly searching for explanations and the reasons for things—actions, life events, life itself.

It is good to ask, but do we really deserve an answer?

We ask this question to gain a deeper understanding and seldom realize that we are actually seeking a deeper peace.

If it is peace that we lack, help us to see that we should be searching our hearts and our true motives, for what resides within us is either the source of peace and contentment or the source of frustration, strife, or depression.

Additional understanding will do nothing to heal a heart that is filled with darkness.

Work with us today, with those who need it, and reveal and heal.

Help those who seek a change of heart to receive what they need to gain the peace and security they desire, not because they deserve it but because they long to be Your child.

Let each of us strive to be not the change we want to see in this world but the change You want to see in this world.

Why? It is beyond explanation and our comprehension. The simplest explanation is love, and even real love transcends explanation. For if we love with a reason, it is conditional. If it is conditional, it is not love.

That simple thought grows even more when we recall that God is love!

Amen.

Day 33

Today's prayer: Lord . . .

Order our days . . .

Our to-do lists are often longer than the day provides. Some things are important and others are not. Even worse, the order in which we believe we should work is wrong. At best it is chaotic and demanding. It distracts us from the things we should be doing.

We long for peace and comfort. Help us to see that lasting and true peace only comes through You.

Order our days . . .

Make our to-do lists into "to do Your will" lists.

Order our days . . .

Put "service to You" at the top of the list in all we do, never to be replaced by any other item. Let every item on the list be done in love.

Order our days . . .

Amen.

Day 34

Today's prayer: Lord . . .

The greatest success ever experienced in this world came from a death—Your death.

We desire success and victory, but not at the cost of death. There is a lesson we can learn from Your death and victory. In order for us to be truly successful, we need to figuratively die to get past what stands in our way.

"Unless a person loses their life . . ."

We are not perfect and always have room for improvement. In losing those aspects of ourselves that stand in our way and act only to hold us back, we create a better, ever-improving version of ourselves, which is the greatest success we could ever achieve.

Show us those aspects of our lives, small or large, that work to hold us back. Help us to replace each of those aspects with others better aligned with Your purpose for us!

Amen.

Day 35

Today's prayer: Lord . . .

We greet this day with love.

Every time we see a friend or someone special, we greet them. We avoid and ignore those people we don't like.

Then there are those people we do not know as friend or foe, and we treat them with indifference.

Most of this behavior is limited to our interactions with people, or so we think. . . .

We greet those people because we love them, and we welcome them into our moment.

Help us to see that this extends beyond our interactions with people, into every aspect of our heart and mind.

Help us to see that we often allow knowledge, feelings, and situations into our moments that do not deserve to be there. In allowing them we unknowingly are saying we love them.

We begin today by greeting the day with love. Let it blanket all that we do and say.

Let that love guide our discernment and actions so that nothing undeserving of our love enters our lives.

Keep us from unwittingly inviting that which intends only to destroy us into even a moment of presence in our lives so that our days are filled with love, joy, peace, and abundance.

We greet this day with love.

Amen.

Day 36

Today's prayer: Lord . . .

We can find many wonderful lessons in nature. One beautiful life lesson can be seen if we look at the river and the seas where You once walked .

Farthest south is a body of water aptly called the Dead Sea. It is the "end of the river" and is lifeless. Nothing flows through it; it takes all it can get and returns nothing. As a result, over time it has grown so salty that any life that flows into it from the river to the north dies.

Farther north is the Sea of Galilee. The water it contains is the same water as the Dead Sea. It is different, though; it is teeming with life! Water from the river flows into it and out of it. It gives as much as it receives, sometimes even more. Sea level rises and falls. Sometimes it looks as though it will dry up, but it was a sea with an inlet and an outlet long before man walked this earth and will still be a sea at the end of time.

We pray for life and life abundant, yet have we asked ourselves, "Are we living like the Sea of Galilee or are we the Dead Sea?"

Do the blessings that flow into our lives become enhanced by the presence in our moments, and are they then allowed to flow out? Or does it stop when it reaches us and the life that it contains is consumed and destroyed by our saltiness?

We pray today to be living fountains of Your blessings and not drains—or, worse, cesspools.

Help us to see that what we think we need to have a happy life may not be the blessings that we are meant to enhance and share. All else that we need will be added when we "seek first the kingdom."

Order our lives and desires. You promised that You would take care of our needs, and we believe that.

Make us into Seas of Galilee and fountains providing blessings to the world around us, making what we have been given even better for our having them before we share.

Amen.

Day 37

Today's prayer: Lord . . .

Long ago the question was asked of those who followed Your wisdom, "Are you of Peter or Paul?" In other words, "Who is right?" and "What do you believe?"

How childish and narrow-minded of us to think there is just one right way for everyone to think or do anything.

Scientists have convinced themselves that what they think is the truth. Doctors believe that they have the only answers. Psychologists see only one way to resolve issues. Schools teach but one answer, churches but one theology.

Sadly, many wonderful alternatives and opportunities for growth are rejected and, more important, lives are excluded.

The question of "Peter or Paul" remains at the very foundation of our lives. Sadly, we often do the same as those "professing to be wise have become but fools."

We live with but one perspective, believing it to be the only truth. We wallow in mediocrity and miss the fact that what we believe may also be what is holding us there.

Open our eyes. Broaden our vision. Help us to see that the answers to life's questions are as varied as those who ask. And help us to change as we grow.

The right answer for one may mean certain death for another. Make us constantly aware of this.

Life may be a test, but this exam has many right answers. What matters is what fits with our moment and that it brings us closer to serving You as You intended.

Let us be ever aware that if we are meant to be the answers to others' questions, let them not be our answers but Yours—specifically for those we are with.

Keep us from the folly of the "professed wise." Let us never become narrow in our view, but help us to listen and build upon the knowledge of others.

It is not for us to tear down or reject the knowledge of others but to provide alternatives so that in the interactions learning occurs. For we may find that it was not that we were called to help another, but they were called to help us!

We do not follow Peter or Paul. We follow the truth that You have given us, and the truth has set us free!

Thank You!

Amen.

Day 38

Today's prayer: Lord . . .

"There is a season . . ."

We often pray for things to be different so that we can be happy or feel safer. We pray for differences and refuse to change.

Isn't it strange that we haven't considered that the reason we feel the way we do is the way it will be until we change?

Sometimes we change and want our prior life restored, keeping what we acquired through the change. And then we pray for things to go back to the way they were.

Help us to see that, at this moment, all that we are and all that we have is because of the decisions we have made and the actions we have taken.

We are fully responsible for our situation. Life has unfolded just as it was meant to given that simple formula.

We have what we have and are what we are, for all that we have or have not done with what we have been given.

If we pray for difference and do not change, there will be no change, as corny as that sounds.

Help us to realize that we are where we are. For that reason, our destination is not somewhere out there. It is today, and we have arrived! It has been determined; it can't be any different.

Tomorrow will be built by what happens today. There exist infinite possibilities.

The journey that many refer to is in the past. It can't be changed. It has given us what we have.

Let us see that it's not the journey, but in fact it's the destination!

It is about today and what we do with what we have become.

Every destination is in fact a crossroad leading to tomorrow. If we desire something different at this point in our lives, it is a clear message that changes are needed.

If we desire more for all that we have done, then we have to do more. It is what it is for what we did.

Without change, we are deceiving ourselves and there will be no change.

Today we stand at yet another crossroad and pray for the strength to become the new creature that we need to be in order to receive the things we pray for tomorrow.

Turn the page in this chapter of our lives and let us see that there is an entirely different story ahead of us. We no longer desire to write it on our own. Inspire us and write it with us. Change us.

With Your help we can and will live happily ever after, in but another "new season." A new tomorrow.

Amen.

Day 39

Today's prayer: Lord . . .

Fantasy . . . "Get real!"

This life has placed so many things in front of us: unfinished business from our past, commitments and responsibilities, hopes, dreams, temporary pain and suffering, challenges. . . . The list is long and seemingly endless. Some are real and have purpose, and others are not.

Sorting the real from the fantasy is difficult. Help us to "get real."

Our days are numbered. Regardless, we have much to do and have little extra time and resources to waste on the meaningless or hopeless, much less on fantasies.

Enough is enough! Clear our lives of anything that does not serve You. Make our lives entirely real. Work with us so that we become partners in our personal realities.

The world tells us to chase our dreams and live our fantasies, which often become self-created lies because we neglect to listen to You. We will only live authentically happy and be truly successful when we listen to You and when we ask You to be with us today, and help us to get real and live!

Amen.

Day 40

Today's prayer: Lord . . .

Teach us to pray!

Words You have heard in the past and a question that we need to ask, for it is through our prayers and meditations that we draw closer to You and our real meaning.

When You taught here on earth, You gave us an example. Many say this prayer often and miss the lesson You intended to teach. Help us to see that effective prayer and meditation has four ingredients:

Adoration. "Hallowed be thy name."

Confession. "Forgive us our trespasses."

Thanksgiving. "For this is Your kingdom and glory."

. . . and . . .

Sanctification. "Give us this day . . . and lead us not into . . ."

It's easy for us to remember these elements. They spell the word "ACTS"!

Help us to be constantly reminded that prayer and meditation are not passive but active. It is our acts that make our prayers meaningful. How we pray and what we say are meaningless unless we act!

Help us today to become active in our prayer life.

Make our prayers more than words, and enter our lives and this world through us and in us, for we are here and live for Your glory forever and ever.

It is then that our actions make our lives a prayer to You.

Amen.

Day 41

Today's prayer: Lord . . .

There is no denying that we are complex creatures. It seems that our lives grow more complex as each day passes. We pray for our lives to be simpler and often think that a simple life is the answer.

After we realize and accept that You are the king of kings and the master of masters, we need to see that authentic living is the result of a blend of many things at the proper time!

In our impatience we want it all now. In Your loving kindness You often change us one aspect at a time, and even though we know this, we grow impatient.

Help us to faithfully follow Your guidance and change those aspects of our lives that keep us from fully experiencing what You have designed us to be.

Be it one at a time or many, it will not become less complex. It will not be more than we can handle. It will only make our lives more meaningful.

Today we pray that You show us the power that exists in living in Your plan, whether it is simple or full of complexity.

Help us to grasp and hold to the fact that this comes through the simple combination of love and gratitude, for when these two things are present in our lives, our actions change and we touch others' lives.

You are love, and we are grateful. It is in this union that we become new creatures.

And through our perceived complexity and trust in You, You teach us to simply and fully love You, for that is what is "first and foremost," with all of our heart, soul, and mind.

You never promised us that it would be SIMPLE and EASY. You promised that it would be worth it! And when we realize that and act in faith, we can begin changing the world—or at least the part that matters.

AND THAT IS WORTH IT!

Amen.

Day 42

Today's prayer: Lord . . .

"My cup runneth over."

Bucket list: the list of things we want to do or see before we leave this world. Whether we have an official list or not, somehow we all have them. Until we have fulfilled our desires, our buckets seem to remain less than full.

Take us back to the wisdom of the psalmist today and remind us of those things that should really fill our "buckets," for You are our protector and shepherd.

"I shall not want."

You have promised that our every need has been and will be taken care of. First and foremost, many of our "wants" are truly nothing more than leaks in our buckets that drain us from true abundance.

"He leads me . . ."

Many search for their mission, purpose, and direction, and they search in vain. Where do we go to receive our mission and purpose?

To You. You lead me!

"I fear no evil."

With You for us and us following Your direction, who can be against us? Help us to always remember that our buckets must contain an ample amount of boldness in Your name.

"Your rod and staff comfort me."

We desire peace and a comfortable life. Help us to see that these are possible only when we act as Your children in a gentleness of spirit, a kindness toward all creatures large and small. Help us to act with love and follow You through the good and the painful.

"Surely goodness and mercy will follow me all the days of my life."

Of all things, Your goodness and mercy are beyond measure. If we have but one thing on our list to fill our buckets, it is that. As we look across our lives, help us to realize that our buckets "overflow already."

Thank You!

And help us to see that which we can't retain, that which overflows, needs to touch the lives of others.

If we are to have a bucket list, let it be of things, experiences, and events that overflow, touch the lives of others, and bring them closer to You.

Let our buckets be filled to overflowing with Your grace, mercy, kindness, compassion, and love. Can anything better flow from us and touch the lives of others?

Amen.

Day 43

Today's prayer: Lord . . .

You told us that there will always be wars and rumors of wars. You also told us that the real battles being fought are beyond our regular perception, between powers and principalities, things unseen.

One of those wars is fought within ourselves. These battles rage so silently that we do not even realize that they are being fought. It is the battle between our mind and our heart, our logic and knowledge versus our desire to grow.

There is a duality in our very nature and, by purpose, in our design: that of our mind and that of our heart. Each has a purpose that serves us and You.

Our heart is the realm of passion, love, and growth. It is what makes us do what we do. Our heart controls our actions; we will always act from our heart.

Our hearts are pure and focused and naïve, made so by You. You have created in us "a clean heart."

The purpose of our mind is survival. Its purpose is to keep us alive, to survive. It learns and from that knowledge works diligently to convince our heart to act upon "logic" to keep us normal, often through perception and deception.

Our mind's purpose is to keep us in our place. Our heart's purpose is to make us grow. Our mind works to deceive the heart, and our heart strives to remain pure and take us higher and closer to You.

This is the answer to Paul's paradox of doing what he doesn't want and not doing what he wants. It is our own deception; this is the real silent battle.

You are in control of us if we let You be. We pray that You take control of our entire being—mind and heart.

Help us to grow where growth is needed and "stay put" in areas where we need to stay put. Make us creatures of passion, Your passion, setting us on the path that takes up where You left off.

Let all that we say and do be done so in love. Let not one word or act create strife, controversy, or dissention. Let all that we do be worthy of a child of God.

The war that is being fought within us will always rage. Victory comes one battle at a time. Let every battle that we fight lead us to the day when we hear, "Good job, faithful servant."

Amen.

Day 44

Today's prayer: Lord . . .

Size doesn't matter. As we ponder the vastness of the universe, it overwhelms our simple minds. Even traveling to the nearest planet would take months, and then we'd have to be going faster than we have ever gone.

Then there is light, the ultimate speed limit at 186,000 miles per second. It takes light a second and a half to travel from the moon to the earth. The light from the sun takes more than eight minutes to travel from it to us. The light from the next nearest star takes five years.

Light traveling across the known universe takes nearly 28 billion years, and You are beyond that! In truth, size means nothing to You.

How long does it take our thoughts and prayers to get to You? The answer is amazing. . . .

No time at all!

You are timeless and beyond our limits. Help us to see that.

As we think of the universe, our thoughts immediately go to its farthest limits of it. As we think of You, our thoughts go beyond, directly and immediately to You, unrestricted by time or distance.

Our thoughts and prayers traverse and fill the universe immediately and constantly. That is amazing! It is why "every head in heaven turns at the mention of Your name."

Help us to be ever mindful of this, and let that reminder guide our thoughts and prayers in such ways that what we think and say is good, true, and beautiful always—not just in prayers but in all things.

If goodness and mercy are to follow us, let them flow from us first and fill heaven and earth with praise and gratitude to You. And let not a single thought waver from that call.

Let the world, Your world, be better and filled with goodness for the thoughts, prayers, and acts that we do—with You, through You, and for You.

Amen.

Day 45

Today's prayer: Lord . . .

Where do we start? Many of our prayers focus only on our needs and requests for Your help, intervention, and blessings. We pray for and need . . .

Help with our jobs . . .

Health and healing . . .

Peace, comfort, and security.

We pray for others and for ourselves.

Today we put all those aside, as difficult as it may be to do so, and we start the day with a song of praise and a simple prayer of gratitude to You!

This is where every day should begin. It is a firm foundation upon which our prayers are answered. A day that starts with praise and gratitude will flavor all of our thoughts and our actions. It will flavor all of our prayers.

"For this is the day the Lord has made. Let us be glad and rejoice."

Take the burdens and pains and fears from us, even for just a moment, and let us experience the purity, cleanliness, and excitement that flow from the realization that You are always with us.

Help us to make praise and gratitude more than a morning thing. Make it into an "all the time thing," regardless of the situations we are in.

We are unstoppable when driven by heartfelt praise and gratitude.

Today we praise You and just say thank You for all that You've done for us despite all that we've done—to ourselves and to You.

Amen.

Day 46

Today's prayer: Lord . . .

The path to peace is lifelong, for the real peace that we seek can only be had at the end of our roads, and our destination of true peace and acceptance comes to us only after a lifetime of living.

Yet while we walk through life we encounter many curves, twists and turns.

That's life!

One of these "curves" that we will encounter is called disbelief.

Open our eyes to reality and bring us comfort in our encountering this curve. Make our clearer vision see your work through us such that our faith to navigate this curve exceed this diversion.

There is the "turn" of anger, and it is sharp and long. Help us to see that anger is a by-product of selfishness. Give us the focus on what matters and the anger will subside, and the road will again straighten.

On our path is a "hill" called bargaining. Help us to realize that compromise is and is not the answer, that the only answer is love for one another.

Often we find a "tunnel" that becomes dark with sadness. This comes when we see that this path is real and all we have, but there is a light at the other end.

Then we encounter the "slippery slope" called acceptance. We often wrongly believe that we have reached our destination, but it is not the end of our journey—just a calm acceptance of the moment at hand.

Help us to remember that these twists and turns are as much a part of the road as the road itself. That is life, and those curves, turns, hills, slopes and tunnels of our path describe the path itself. And anytime we face one of these challenges, we may travel the same curve or hill or slope many times over wherever we are. It's good and right for each person, but not necessarily for anyone else.

Help us to see that we are where we are and it's okay, and that others are where they are. It's okay, for our duty in life is to accept where we are and, through love, help others on the same road without judgment or strife.

This is what makes our final destination worth the trip.

Amen.

Day 47

Today's prayer: Lord . . .

Every day is a new beginning, yet it is only in the direst times when we truly realize this. On most days it is our nature to carry our past into the present. The fact that we all do this means that it is part of our intended design and has a purpose.

Common sense tells us that there are things we need to bring into today from yesterday. And there are things that we need to leave behind. Yet, as simple as that thought is, we often carry things that You wish us to leave and leave things that You wish us to carry into today.

Give us the appropriate wisdom so that we choose more wisely and more in keeping with Your will. It is then that we will walk closer to the path You prepared, free from fear and totally secure in our lives, and with those whom we are blessed to be with. We will be doing what we need to do with what we have!

Amen.

Day 48

Today's prayer: Lord . . .

Nothing good comes to us without a cost. A person will not lose weight or become healthier without a change in diet and exercise. Small change, small gains, temporary change, temporary gains.

A person does not receive a wage without work. Menial work, menial pay, part-time work, part-time pay.

A person cannot have a relationship and without giving to and for the other. Small sacrifices are shallow; strong commitments are unstoppable.

These and many other situations show that this is a simple fact of life. Even though it is a fact, many believe and act as if they can get what they want without change, without a cost. Great things come at a high cost. The greater the good, the higher the cost.

Your death showed us that forgiveness could not enter this world without a cost: a death!

Your death.

You saw that the greater the good, the higher the cost!

The greatest gift we could ever receive: Your forgiveness! And You paid the price.

Thank You!

Help us to see that often the cost attached to what we want is not just pocket change or small change; it is real change that requires conscious effort. If we wish for the best, the cost is great. The greater the good, the higher the cost.

Help us to see that in every situation that we are called to fulfill, it may not be easy or cheap, but the cost is worth it.

Let us realize that nothing we are entitles us to anything. It is not what we were or what we are that is of value.

What we have received is what we earned, and that is it.

The future is all about what we do from this day forward. When forgiveness entered the world, our "savings accounts" of actions were cleared out. We are living on credit given by You and through You!

Thank God, for all we deserved from our past was no good. Our world has changed. We have been given the chance to live in abundance and authentic happiness. We can now be victorious in the race of life. Help us to realize that only the winners are the ones worthy of the real trophy. Let us "run our race to win."

Our future is determined by the cost that we pay today, by what we put into it. Our cost is change, but let us not think that our cost is menial coins. It is true change—life change!

In ourselves—our desires, our beliefs, our actions—it is working in Your will, despite what our will tells us. Open our eyes to our deception and let us see that today we are but nothing, but what we can become is also worth it.

Change us from deep inside so that what we seek is nothing more than the result of what we are.

Make the change. Make it lasting. Make it worth it.

Amen.

Day 49

Today's prayer: Lord . . .

We live in a world of rules and restrictions. Every rule, every sanction, every bias, every prejudice does nothing but narrow our freedom.

Rules and laws are here for the lawless and to protect the lawful from those who believe wrongly about freedom. It is sad that people believe freedom means doing what they want. There is nothing further from the truth than that.

You came and made it possible for us to experience real freedom: the freedom to do what is good, true, and beautiful; the freedom to love God with all of our heart, soul, and mind; the freedom to love our neighbors as ourselves.

Help us to see that there is but one freedom: the freedom to do good. All else is deception, which enslaves us to the world. Help us to exercise our real freedom today, made possible only by You.

Extend our freedom and let it touch others' lives with acts that are good, true, beautiful, and selfless in ways, before today, unimaginable.

Amen.

Day 50

Today's prayer: Lord . . .

"And have not love . . ."

"It's all or nothing."

Love . . .

For thousands of years people have pondered the nature of love. It is a condition that is unexplainable, yet we know it when we see it. It is a condition, yet it is not conditional!

We could possess everything in this world, but if we don't have love, we are nothing.

You taught us a simple truth: "God is love." When we combine that truth with the prior observation, how eye-opening. . . .

We work diligently to obtain simple security. We work to amass possessions. We think we will have happiness when we get what we want, but if we do not have love, we will never know happiness. Could it be that we are working for the wrong reasons?

Open our eyes today and let us see what was really meant by "Seek first the kingdom of God [love] and His righteousness, and all these things will be added to you."

Let us not be like the world in its ignorant and vain attempts to create many levels and definitions of love. There is but one love, and it is God. Like God it is unconditional; it is unchanging; it is unshakable. It is all or nothing.

If we think that love varies with the situation or comes with conditions or changes, we are deceiving ourselves and, sadly, those who believe our hollow words.

Love does not serve the "self" in the smallest fashion. It does not have its own terms and conditions.

Help us not only know love when we see it but *be* love.

Help us to see that love is an "all or nothing" proposition, and we will not experience it until we go "all in." For in truth it is all or nothing, just as You showed us when You walked this earth because You went "all in."

Make this simple sentence ring in our hearts with meaning. Seek first love and *all* things will come to you. We are "all in."

Amen.

Day 51

Today's prayer: Lord . . .

We are so fragile and self-focused.

At a moment's notice . . .

We can go from happy to devastated.

We can go from hopeless to elated.

We can go from living to dead.

Yet You, Your love, and Your compassion and caring never change.

It's a fact: Things change.

It's a fact: You don't!

It's a fact: What changes doesn't matter.

It's a fact: What doesn't change matters.

We thank You for these truths. Help us to see these facts in a new light and reveal all that we see for the truth that our beliefs really carry. For it is what we believe that controls our actions and reactions. If what we believe varies, how we react will vary also.

Build our house of belief on "the rock," a firm and solid foundation, so that when the inevitable storms of life come upon us, our house of life will stand . . .

Unaffected . . .

Unchanged . . .

Unharmed . . .

By the fact that what matters doesn't change, and what we believe only grows stronger.

Amen.

Day 52

Today's prayer: Lord . . .

"Let every word that comes from our mouths . . ."

Help us today to see the power of the spoken word. Words are more powerful than the sword, for the sword can only hurt a person physically, but words can inflict permanent damage on both heart and soul.

Our spoken words can soothe or they can wound.

Our words can lift spirits or they can drive others down.

Our words can serve others selflessly or they can serve us selfishly.

Our words are verbal actions emanating from our hearts.

Our true nature and intent become evident in our words.

Words are an open window into our true nature. Make us fully aware of this. What we say is what lies deep within. Change our words so that they reflect and represent You more and more each and every day.

Help us to go beyond choosing our words wisely to the very source of our words: our heart!

Let us look at the real messages carried by our words and see what we need to change. Then give us the strength, ability, and desire to do so.

Each day, let more and more words that come from us be from You and touch the hearts of our listeners in ways that heal, uplift, comfort, and serve rather than hurt, scar, attack, degrade, and damage, for the latter is not of You.

Don't change just our words, but change our hearts so that we do not have to worry about what we say, knowing that it is always for the greater good.

For when the greater good is served, our good is served— and, most important, You are served.

Amen.

Day 53

Today's prayer: Lord . . .

We have a popular saying: "It is what it is." We most often use it as a statement of surrender and submission to the conditions at hand. And most often we fail to realize that in every life event, it can also be the highest form of praise!

Let this simple saying take on an entirely new meaning to us today! You and the universe know each of us better than we know ourselves. You know our real needs better than we know ourselves. We are designed to survive and are not given any situation that we cannot handle to Your glory.

"It is what it is" because You love us and wish for us to grow.

Help us to remember this today, and if we are moved to say those words, let them be in praise of You and Your love. Let these words drive us in ways that show Your glory and victory!

Amen.

Day 54

Today's prayer: Lord . . .

You once told the people around You, "Let the dead tend to the dead."

As cold and heartless as that sounded, a quiet message resounds within. Our lives are about the loving and the lives of those we love.

Help us to look to one another and grow ever stronger through our selfless love for one another. Help us to put our petty issues and feelings aside, lifting up others with the unique talents, strengths, and gifts we have been given.

Together let us show the world around us what it means to be part of a prayer family. And most important, help our "circle of love" to grow ever larger each day!

Together we can change the world—or at least the part that matters—to You, for You, and for those who need Your love!

Amen.

Day 55

Today's prayer: Lord . . .

We often forget that there is a vast difference between what we know and what we believe. Help us to see that we only act on what we believe.

Many people say they believe in You, but their day-to-day actions tell a different story. They simply know of You, if that.

Words are from our mind, actions from our heart. Help us to look deeply into our hearts today and reflect on what is really there. Let us open the door to "what we believe" by constant awareness of our actions and how they carry the real message to the world around us.

Let not our frail and inaccurate knowledge stand in the way of our belief. Keep our knowledge from deceiving and controlling us in ways contrary to Your will.

Make believing in You as natural, embedded, and as important as our belief that breathing is crucial to our life, so that we may better serve You and those who are in need.

Amen.

Day 56

Today's prayer: Lord . . .

The most beautiful statues of stone are not built. They start as a large block of stone, and the artisan chips away at the rock, removing everything that is not part of the final masterpiece.

Let us see that we too are works of the Master's hands. For us to become the vision that You see in us, it is often not a matter of what we acquire but what is removed from the rough block that we currently are.

Let our prayer today and that prayer in which You join with us be to remove those things that stand in our way of fully realizing the plan that You have for us.

Remove all of the imperfections and blemishes.

Heal the hurts and scars from the past.

Smooth the animosity that creates the rough exterior.

Shape us so that we stand as yet another example of the miraculous work that You do in individuals' lives.

Let us be a living masterpiece of Your glory and work, not to our benefit but in answer to the call to love others so that they may also become living statues of Your supreme love and caring.

Amen.

Day 57

Today's prayer: Lord . . .

"Let your light so shine."

It is in the darkest of times when the tiniest light can make the biggest impact. You told us to never hide our light. But what is our light?

Light, from the world's perspective, is simply an energy. Our light is not that light, but it is an energy. It is the energy of our personal existence. It is the energy of our true meaning and purpose.

Some of us light the world with our smiles, some of us with our love. Some of us light the world with our caring, while others shine with knowledge.

Each of us has a special light. It is the light we were given, and given with a purpose. Our light is what makes us who we are!

The darkness has attacked that light and, for many, caused them to hide and protect it.

Let us not be afraid of the dark. Help us to boldly shine as You intended.

Our light may be bright or it may be dim, but what we have we will shine for You and, most important, to Your glory. For it has been said that "it is better to light a small candle than to curse the darkness."

For us it is better to be that small candle of hope, comfort, security, or love than to allow someone to be in darkness.

Help us to hold true to our light. Give us the awareness, wisdom, strength, confidence, and love to be a light unto a dark world and to always shine hope on the hopeless when they need us most—just as You did when You walked the earth.

Amen.

Day 58

Today's prayer: Lord . . .

"Unto us a child is born."

When You came into this world, You came as an answer to a specific problem. You and Your life and death proved to be that answer.

In our narrow view of this amazing event, we miss another important and life-shaping message for us. Help us to see it today and let this message sink deep into our heart so that we never forget it.

Not unlike You, we came into this world as helpless babes, with the pain of childbirth announcing our arrival. Not unlike You, we were helpless. And not unlike You, we were brought here as an answer to a problem to the world that was to be fulfilled at an appointed time.

Although ours is not as large or universal as Yours, each of us is here as an answer. We have been shaped by Your loving hands and protected, to grow to be that answer.

Help us to be ever mindful of this, and as we walk our path, let every step we take be with purpose and intent, focused on the answer that we are here to be.

Let us not become fixated on finding the problem until the time is right. We too are here to fulfill a purpose. Big or small, that helpless baby came with hope.

Let us not fail in Your glory and praise, so that others too will come to You and grow.

Amen.

Day 59

Today's prayer: Lord . . .

There are times when we should live quietly. There are times when we should live with such passion that the world cannot keep us quiet.

We are not meant to live just one way or the other. There is a time and a place for both. We are often tempted to act in ways contrary to Your will.

There are also times when we have no choice. It is difficult for us to know how to be in each situation.

Our words may carry a message, but it is our actions that carry the truth.

"Let us love God with all our heart."

"Let us love our neighbor as ourselves."

"Let us love one another, for love is of God."

Help us to see that, in all things, love is our trumpet that announces Your entry into and Your presence in us, and in the world at large!

Help us to act and speak wisely, knowing, saying, and doing the proper thing at the proper time!

Most important, help us to always and in all ways act and speak in love. It is then that we go from "living loudly" to how we should actually be—"loving loud"!

Amen.

Day 60

Today's prayer: Lord . . .

We are creatures of mistakes. We are built to fail and heal. That is an important part of life and learning.

Thank You for failure. Thank You for healing, for without it we would not live long enough to reap the harvest of this wonderful gift of learning and growth.

Help us to realize that we can fail in an instant, and it can take years to heal. Let all of our actions be guided by this sobering awareness, and when we by chance or design fail, give us the patience and persistence to heal and learn.

We know that failure is inevitable. Healing is also inevitable and is the gift that You give all of Your creatures freely.

We humbly accept that gift, and in gratitude we thank You for allowing us to live and learn in Your Glory and to our growth.

Amen.

Day 61

Today's prayer: Lord . . .

Events in our lives often raise the question "What was the purpose?"

Other times we question the entire purpose of our own lives. It's a natural part of living to seek these answers; knowing and understanding the purpose of anything gives us a sense of focus and meaning. It calms our mind and soothes our soul.

We do not need the answers to these questions as much as we need Your peace and assurance. It is what we truly seek and it is what You promised.

As we start the day, we should focus our thoughts, words, and deeds on these two things: What has been and is and will come is simply because You love us. What we were and are and will be is because we love You and You love us.

It is no more complex than that. In all cases it is because of love . . . Your love. And most important, You are love!

Focus our hearts on love so that the fruits that spring from our being are acts that show only love. Let us not be distracted by the petty issues of today that distract us from love. Most often the simplest answer is the right one, and the only one.

That answer is love.

Amen.

Day 62

Today's prayer: Lord . . .

There are days when we are torn, and then we are reminded to "count it all joy."

And that "a house divided cannot stand."

And that "a person cannot serve two masters."

The messages and reminders are clear and constant, yet we struggle. Help us to see that where gratitude resides, sadness and regret cannot.

Your message is clear. We cannot be thankful and unhappy at the same time. When sadness knocks at our door, let us answer to that knock with thankfulness. But we do not have to invite that visitor into our house.

Let gratitude reign supreme in our lives, for when we are ruled by this master, our days will be guided in the proper direction and our decisions and actions will always be according to Your will.

Gratitude is the soil from which love can sprout and flourish. The greatest amount of love is found in a garden planted continuously with seeds of gratitude and constantly tended with prayer. The fruits of this garden are all sweet and more than meet our every need.

We must not allow the weeds of sadness into this garden. Make us conscious of how quickly sadness can overtake what was planted and choke the life out of it.

Give us persistent strength to pull these weeds from our lives so that all that grows is good, true, beautiful, and happy.

Amen.

Day 63

Today's prayer: Lord . . .

Calm our fears. We are interesting creatures. We only fear when we believe that we have alternatives. Fear disappears when we see that we have no choice.

Help us to see that we have nothing to fear, for our path was planned long before we breathed our first breath, and every step along that path leads to good.

Calm our fears. Help us to seek and find Your direction step by step, moment by moment, so that we see and believe that we have nothing to fear. We will then live in authentic happiness and in the fullness of love and completeness of gratitude.

". . . the greatest of which is love."

Amen.

Day 64

Today's prayer: Lord . . .

Every sunrise is a reminder of a fresh and glorious restart. When we look to the other side of it from the reverse perspective, we realize that every sunrise is also a sunset. When the sun rises for someone, it is also a sunset for someone on the other side of the same moment.

This is an amazing thought. In order to have a new start, there must also be an ending—and the two are contained within a single moment.

Help us to see this secret and let us not carry yesterday into today. We deeply desire new lives, but that is not possible if we carry yesterday into today. History is in the past; it's gone and will only repeat itself if we bring it forward into today. When things don't change we wonder why we are no different.

Help us to learn and to use this lesson to become the new creature that You promised, living authentically happy for You and Your glory.

Thank You for the sunrise and the sunset, and the fact that the new and the old are actually one and the same.

Amen.

Day 65

Today's prayer: Lord . . .

We ask that You take us, like the apostles, to a deeper understanding of prayer. Let our prayers be more than cries for help and forgiveness or songs of praise and thanksgiving.

Make them the keys that open doors to miracles.

Make them the books of insight and understanding.

Make them the ointment that heals the sick.

Make them the armor that protects us in times of attack.

Make them the paths upon which we walk through life and the light that guides us through dark times.

If we possess but one thing to use to Your glory, make it prayer.

Amen.

Day 66

Today's prayer: Lord . . .

"YOLO." You only live once.

Oh, how we have let the world deceive us. There is one birth and one death, and every moment in between is a chance to live our lives to the fullest by leaving every moment better, in gratitude, for having been given the chance to participate in it.

Every moment contains two doors, and we have the keys to both. We can open the door and unleash strife and discord, or we can open the door of love and kindness and caring.

The doors are clearly marked. Our choices are not accidents.

Help us to search our hearts and understand why we open the doors that we choose. In doing so we will choose the right door more often and leave lives better each and every day.

Amen.

Day 67

Today's prayer: Lord . . .

Help us to stay focused on today. Thoughts from yesterday can be filled with anger, sadness, remorse, regret, and guilt. These only distract us from experiencing the moment to its fullest. Thoughts of tomorrow may bring fear, worry, anxiety, and frustration, distracting us from today. Yesterday and tomorrow can be our enemies, working to enslave us.

You came to set us free. Help us to realize that this freedom comes from living fully in today. Let us not be drawn back to thoughts of the past or future, but instead keep our eyes and hearts fixed upon You.

In doing so we are set free to live fully to Your glory!

Amen.

Day 68

Today's prayer: Lord . . .

Seeking a life of prayer is one of the highest aspirations, yet there is one that stands above every pursuit:

Give us the ability and awareness to be the answer to prayers.
Touch the lives of others—our friends, family, and strangers—though us, making their lives better through our experience wisdom, love, and caring.

Those gifts You have given to us freely, to serve others and, most important, YOU!

Amen.

Day 69

Today's prayer: Lord . . .

Make the prayer that we say today more than words.

Make today's prayer a realization that we are thankful for being where we are and able to pray.

Make us aware of the many things we should be grateful for.

Make us aware of those things we didn't receive because of the ultimate harm they would have caused us.

Make us aware of the protection You have provided.

Make us aware that these thing and events are not just in the past but also here and now!

Make us aware of the love that exists in our lives.

Overwhelm us with all the awareness of the awe and wonder that we have missed in our shortsighted living. Then move us to share that gratitude and love from today onward—to Your praise, to Your glory, and with our simple gratitude.

Amen.

Day 70

Today's prayer: Lord . . .

We often pray for peace. Some pray for release from guilt and depression. Some pray for release from anxiety and fear.

Although we desire peace in the present moment, we do not realize that the things we seek release from are not even conditions of the present moment. If we have those conditions, it is our fault.

Help us to see that if we are looking to rid ourselves of depression and guilt, we are living in the past.

Help us to see that if we are looking for release from fear and anxiety, we are living in the future. Peace and happiness come to those who focus on the present moment.

You have given us that ability to focus, free from our past failures, free from future worries.

In one word: faith!

Today we ask for the faith that will free us from the bondage of guilt and regret, fear and anxiety. Help us to use our faith to focus on the present moment so that we can fully realize the peace that we seek.

To Your glory and service . . .

Amen.

Day 71

Today's prayer: Lord . . .

It is easy to pray for those people we care about, but it is much harder for us to pray for those we harbor ill feelings toward.

Help us to embrace Your life and Your guidance today so that we act in ways that show love to our enemies.

Bless those who curse us.

Do good to those who treat us with hate.

Pray for those who persecute us.

Real love is shown when we act with no regard for what we will receive in return for the love we give.

Let our love go beyond words and feelings to actions. Do not let our feelings and beliefs stand in the way of the love that we show the world. Any act that withholds love from another is an act of judgment.

Help us to remember: "Judge not, lest you be judged."

Help us to put this into a transforming context: "Love, lest you not be loved."

Help us to always show the level of love that is needed in every moment and not let our selfish desires or our judgmental biases stand in the way of fully experiencing Your presence, which is manifest in the love that we bring into the moment through our actions.

Amen.

Day 72

Today's prayer: Lord . . .

We all seek meaningful relationships for many different reasons. A major source of this hunger is our need for completeness.

Completeness comes with a cost. Regardless of the relationship, our true meaning ultimately comes from the fullness of our relationship with You. It is from that beginning that fullness springs, whether with You or with people of this world.

Let us see that there is no such thing as half of a relationship. In every case, the cost of a true relationship is all or nothing—heart, mind, body. If one is missing, it is not a relationship. If we believe that we can have meaning and withhold one or more, we deceive ourselves and, worse, the one whom we have deceived into believing in the commitment.

Make us "all in" people.

Make our commitments full and complete.

Let our first commitment be to You so that Your glory can be shown through our love, and so that others will benefit from what we have learned.

Amen.

Day 73

Today's prayer: Lord . . .

Give all those who have given up, a fighting chance.

Strengthen their will.

Heal their wounds and lack of faith.

Take control of their minds and bodies, fill them with reassurance, give them peace.

Make them triumphant over disease, broken relationships, loneliness, sadness, and guilt.

We look from you to do this, because only you can make this miracle of life happen.

Amen.

Day 74

Today's prayer: Lord . . .

You have given us prayer as the most wonderful of gifts.

It is the most powerful medicine against our sicknesses of mind, body and soul.

It is the glue that mends broken relationships.

It is a soothing lotion.

It is a song of praise.

Most of all, it is a sonnet of gratitude.

Let our prayers totally reflect the depth of the gift, as we make our lives prayers to you!

Amen.

Day 75

Today's prayer: Lord . . .

As we go through this life, there are things we enjoy doing and things we don't. How we feel about our responsibilities should not matter in our doing them. It is all part of Your plan.

You told us, "Whatever you do, do as if asked directly by God." As we consider this we realize that we are part of Your plan and have been called by God to do what we are doing.

Help us to work with the passion and enthusiasm that we should so that our gratitude shows in our actions and our love shines so that others see what leads people to true abundance and peace.

Amen.

Day 76

Today's prayer: Lord . . .

Before I ask for anything else, let me thank You for the blessings that I have already been given.

Thank You for another chance to share your glory.

Thank You for my family, those by blood and those with whom I relate because of You.

Thank You for the strength that I have, to accomplish my daily tasks.

Thank You for the safety that You provide.

Thank You for all answered prayers and for those that remain unanswered.

Thank you for Your Love, Patience and Grace, for without them, I am nothing!

Amen.

Day 77

Today's prayer: Lord . . .

"Even the hairs on our heads . . ."

You know our every need. You provide for and protect those who love and follow You. We were created to love You fully in a way unique to us.

We need to be who we are with gratitude for what we've been given and hope in what we need. We thank You for both.

Blind our eyes and emotions from those things that work only to distract us. Let us see that we can do what we have been called to do with the meager amount of love and trust that we have.

We lay our every need before You and trust that they will be handled.

From this will spring more and deeper love and gratitude, and exactly what You so desire from us.

Amen.

Day 78

Today's prayer: Lord . . .

Of all the things that You give to us, the greatest gift is love. Although many will deny it, we were built to love. We seek to love and to be loved. We seek to fulfill those needs. Sadly, we often settle for that which is not real.

Many will selfishly and desperately seek any form of love to fill that hunger.

Many will use that need for love to control and manipulate those who are seeking. Others will create and live in fantasies, hiding from reality.

We pray with gratitude for those who have real love, and we pray for those who lack love.

Help us to recognize the source of this powerful gift fully and to never lose this realization, for all things will pass away but love stands eternal.

We pray that we will stand eternally with You . . .

IN LOVE . . .

AS LOVE . . .

Amen.

Day 79

Today's prayer: Lord . . .

We often have been told that the world exists to deceive us. This is not entirely true. More often it is we who are deceivers— of ourselves, who are the deceived!

Help us to see that the hardest person for us to be honest with is ourselves.

Give us true honesty.

Open our eyes and let us see ourselves as You see us.

It is then and only then that we will make the changes that You long to see in our lives, which allow us to fully experience the life You promised.

Amen.

Day 80

Today's prayer: Lord . . .

Please put an extra touch of healing on those who need it.

Calm relationships and give their bodies the ability to confront the diseases that inflict them.

Help them to overcome their suffering and rise victorious over their struggles.

Be more than a light at the end of the tunnel by lighting their entire walk.

Show them your light, so that their darkness is removed.

Let them feel a renewed energy to serve you.

Amen.

Day 81

Today's prayer: Lord . . .

Your story of the prodigal son carries a message that many people miss, as we do with many others of Your lessons. Today we look deeper at Your story.

The father waits patiently at home while the son is out in the world. Realizing his folly, the son leaves the city and begins the journey home. As the son approaches, the father sees the son en route home and runs to him.

Your message is clear. The father waits, not for our arrival but for us to take the first step in the right direction. And then he runs to us.

Remove our deception that we have to wait for the achievement and see that You simply wait for the sincere move in the right direction.

Move us, dear Lord, to take the real step toward home.

We know that we won't find You there, but You are with us all the way home.

Amen.

Day 82

Today's prayer: Lord . . .

We pray for Your help. We pray for Your blessings. Our prayers are focused on what we can get rather than what we need to do to make a difference in our lives.

Today we ask that You make us true prayer warriors. Give us the strength and means to help others and the motivation to do it.

Make us a blessing to others. Move us to be that blessing without expectation of return.

Direct our vision and actions outward so that we act in ways that make a difference in this world and in the lives of those who matter most to You.

Use us as defenders of those who need Your love and protection.

Help us to be less concerned with our own needs and totally focused on what You have planned for us to do today.

Amen.

Day 83

Today's prayer: Lord . . .

Open new doors for me.

Shine Your light where there is darkness.

Put Your strength where I am weak.

Mend those things that I have broken.

Bind those things in my life that intend to slow my growth.

Heal what is sick.

Most important, renew the LOVE that was instilled in me from the very beginning and give me the peace that comes as a result of knowing You.

Amen.

Day 84

Today's prayer: Lord . . .

Be with those who need help and are struggling to make sense of their lives.

Help those with heavy hearts.

Give them the peace that provides the needed understanding.

Let them see that oftentimes it is simply "knowing that You are God" that is more than enough.

Remind them that the past is totally forgiven and has passed.

Let them see that You have gone into tomorrow to prepare a place for them.

Focus them on the moment at hand and fill it with love.

They need You. Be with them today.

Amen.

Day 85

Today's prayer: Lord . . .

Renew the fire in our lives.

Remind us of the joy that we felt when we first found You.

Let us NEVER forget the purity of life and living with You., that we had when we realized Your place in our lives.

Protect us from the woes that we encounter by our submission to the ills of this world.

Regardless of our age, we are but helpless children.

Without You we are nothing. From dust, we came and to dust we shall return

In the meantime, allow us to serve as You planned.

For we do this in Love and Gratitude and most of all, to your Glory and Praise.

Amen.

Day 86

Today's prayer: Lord . . .

We ask to have the persistence and focus that You had when You walked this earth.

Help us to see what You planned for us clearly.

Make straight our path and take us into the lives of those who need us.

Make us an answer to prayer and a miracle for those who need it.

Let them see that it was You who brought us to them, given You and only You the glory and gratitude.

We walk this path so that in the end we hear, "Good job, faithful servant."

Amen.

Day 87

Today's prayer: Lord . . .

Remove our worries or at least put them in their proper place.

Help us to see that the best response to stressful situations is to look to you for answers or to give them to you, then let go.

Help us to act as if we were the answer and to pray as if the only answer was from you.

It is this combination of action and prayer that will relieve every worry and keep us on the path that you planned for us.

Let us see that worry is nothing more than our hearts telling us to pray more and work harder.

Amen.

Day 88

Today's prayer...Lord...

You are our Father.

We are offspring of our earthly parents and carry their genetics.

We are told that we look like our fathers or mothers.

We are told that we act or sound like them.

We may have their eyes or body builds.

We may carry their actions into the present.

Whatever!

Help us to remember that we are your children too.

Make our words and deeds such that when people look at us.

They see you.

We want your eyes, to see those who need your love.

We need your heart to spur us to meaningful actions.

We need your voice to say the rights things.

We need your love to touch the hearts of others as they need to be touched.

We need your hands and feet...that take us to the people who need us now and are healed.

Let it be such that when others see us...they see You and know that it was You who worked in their lives.

Let them say, "You are just like your Father!"

Amen

Day 89

Today's prayer: Lord . . .

Help us to see that we don't need fancy words to pray.

You already know our needs.

We don't need to say our prayer out loud.

You know our hearts and can listen to our most subtle thoughts.

Help us to simply say what we mean and believe.

Our prayers are not for You, but for us.

Make our prayers simple and meaningful.

It is the simple heartfelt prayer that will change the world, or at least the part that matters.

Amen.

Day 90

Today's prayer...Lord...

It is through you that we obtain renewal...

Just as the rain cleanses the earth, your presence in our lives cleans and restores us.

Help us to welcome the rain as a gift.

Help us to welcome the sun as a gift.

Give us the ability to look skyward and feel the soothing touch of each drop and to also look on your presence in both the rain and the sun.

Help us to see all the conditions of life as warming, cleansing and restoring gifts...and never take them for ranted...

Amen

Day 91

Today's prayer: Lord ...

You came and gave the world hope, and it changed.

Thank You.

You gave us the gift of hope, and we changed.

Thank You.

Make us beacons of hope to others and to the world today. Let it be that we are changed with Your hope and that, through our lives, others receive the hope they need to do the same.

It is the hope that we possess in the present that seeds the garden of tomorrow. Plant those seeds within us today and make the harvest bountiful.

Amen.

Day 92

Today's prayer: Lord . . .

We are creatures of habit. It is our habits that define who we are.

Help us to look seriously at ourselves and see who we are from this perspective.

Of all the habits in our lives that we possess, make love the strongest, for with love all our other habits fall into their proper place or fade.

Amen.

Day 93

Today's prayer: Lord . . .

"If things were different."
We pray this often. Sometimes this prayer is warranted, but not as often as it is said.

You made us for a specific purpose, and our desires often lead us away from that. These desires promise something better but seldom deliver.

Teach us to pray more discriminately and to desire change only when it serves You better.

Let our prayers contain more gratitude and thankfulness for what we are.

Help us to realize that in praying for things to be different, we do not gain but lose ourselves.

Instead we pray that You make us more of ourselves, making the differences in this world and its people that we were built to do.

Amen.

Day 94

Today's prayer: Lord . . .

You came so we could have life and live it abundantly. Help us to stop today and take stock of the abundance in our lives.

Do our cups overflow with goodness, love, caring, faith, happiness, and comfort? Or do our cups contain sadness, fear, anger, hate, and strife?

Work diligently with us to make our lives and their abundance nothing but sweet nectar. The truth is that it is only our abundance that touches others.

Make all our abundance good, and of You, for in that abundance we bless others' lives and we are blessed by You.

Amen.

Day 95

Today's prayer: Lord . . .

Help us to see that prayers are more than words.

Make our prayers into hugs for those who we can't be with.

Make our prayers a hand that wipes tears of those with sadness.

Make our prayers songs of excitement and praise.

Make our lives prayers to you!

Amen.

Day 96

Today's prayer: Lord . . .

There is nothing that we have that is not a gift.

Thank You.

Help us to find a deeper understanding of that truth. Help us to realize not only more of what You have given us, but also those wonderful gifts in our lives that we don't recognize: our hidden talents, the people who support us, our situations. . . . The list is endless.

Make gratitude to You the glue of a more abundant life, for the things, people, and situations we do not appreciate will be taken away. Then the gift changes from a blessing to a lesson, and for that we are also thankful.

All of these gifts are borrowed, and all will be returned at some time.

Amen.

Day 97

Today's prayer: Lord ...

Help us to remember that in all cases prayer is the answer.

When we are sad, prayer gives us comfort.

When we are alone, prayer assures us that You are with us.

At the lowest point in our lives, prayer gives us hope.

In our darkest times, prayer is our light.

When we are weak, prayer is our strength.

Such a wonderful gift, you have given us.

When we see this, let us remember to thank you first!

Amen.

Day 98

Today's prayer: Lord . . .

Where do we start?

Help us to see:

That miracles will happen for those who believe.

That courage comes to those with faith.

Hope comes to those who dream.

Love comes to those who accept.

Forgiveness comes to those who forgive.

For us to receive, we must first give.

For those who seek these things, we ask that you first give them what it takes to receive them.

Amen.

Day 99

Today's prayer: Lord . . .

Your angels once warned Lot's wife not to look back.

The message was clear.

Do not return to your old ways.

Unlike Lot and his family, we are not fleeing a city being destroyed, but we are fleeing a life that was destroying us!

Help us not to look back and only to look forward to the life that is to come.

Amen.

Day 100

Today's prayer: Lord . . .

We often seek things without considering what we want in its entirety.

Today we ask differently and with wisdom.

Make us strong and keep us from being rude and frightening.

Make us kind, yet keep us from being seen as weak.

Make us bold and keep us from becoming a bully.

Make us humble and keep us from becoming shy.

Make us confident and keep us from arrogance.

Make us everything that You have envisioned and keep us from forgetting where it all came from, for anything of value is from You and all of it is for Your glory.

Amen.

Day 101

Today's prayer: Lord . . . .

Today is a day that You have made. In fact, with You all things are made anew. It's a new day, and we pray that it is a happy one.

As we watch children on a playground, we are reminded of Your admonition: "Unless you become as little children . . ."

They laugh. They sing. They enjoy the moment. They revel in the magic of life. They live with untainted faith. They are loved and give love.

We had that once, and for all practical purposes we have lost it. Renew in us a child-like passion for life, all the attributes that make being a child wonderful, and enhance it with the seasoning of adulthood.

You make all things new and wonderful. This is truly the magic of life, and that gift is there for the taking.

Make this new day one of awe, wonder, magic, life, and love, unfettered by distractions.

Let us enjoy the playground You built for us. Remind us to leave it better for our having been allowed to play on it.

Amen.

Day 102

Today's prayer: Lord . . .

You told us to "guard what goes into our hearts," for out of our hearts "come the issues of life."

Our lives are not filled with issues; it is our hearts that are the issue. We will encounter many things, good and bad, throughout our days here.

Help us to not see any situation for the bad it contains and take each one for the good that it will also provide, so that what our heart takes in and contains is only good, and today all of our issues are good ones.

Help us guard our hearts.

Amen.

Day 103

Today's prayer: Lord . . .

Thank You for showing Your strength through those who are loyal to You.

We often miss that Your power is evident to the world in its day-to-day stability, like the consistency of the sunrises and sunsets. Without You the world would fall into chaos, yet You show Your strength through Your ultimate control of nature—like the flood, the parting of the sea, manna from heaven, calming the storms. . . . The list is long and miraculous.

All of these were not to show how strong You are but to help those who loyally served You.

Help us to live our lives such that our love and loyalty to You elicit those miracles, not solely for our benefit but so that Your glory can be shown to this world, and so that more of Your children come to You in love.

Amen.

Day 104

Today's prayer: Lord . . .

You suggested that we pursue the things that make for peace and the things by which one may lift up another. Herein lies one of the secrets of happy and fulfilled living.

Give us the strength to submit our self-directed needs to You so that we can focus on the peace and needs of others.

Your glory and our happiness come not from the work of our strengths but are shown to the world through our weaknesses and Your grace.

Lord, give us the strength to be weak.

Amen.

Day 105

Today's prayer: Lord . . .

Only You know right from wrong. We are not capable of judging the good or bad of another. We do not know Your expectations for them.

Help us to look only at ourselves when we feel the urge to judge, and then help us to look only to You when we feel judged and need forgiveness.

Make this a part of our life and turn it into a growing experience that makes this world better for our having been here.

Amen.

Day 106

Today's prayer: Lord . . .

Put meaning into every moment of our lives today.

Let us go to bed knowing that we have done everything that needed to be done.

Take our worries about tomorrow away so that we rest peacefully, knowing that You are God and that it is all going as you have planned.

The world would have us overwhelmed and distracted.

Keep us focused on the things that You would have us do, for You know what we are capable of more than we know of ourselves.

This is the beginning of a faith that leads us along our intended path.

Amen.

Day 107

Today's prayer: Lord . . .

Help us to see that the greatest test within our lives is to be a blessing to someone who is going through the same storm as we are.

It is often through our giving the answers to others, that we often find the answers for ourselves.

What we see as trials, tribulations and tests are often the answers to our prayers.

When our eyes are opened to this wonderful truth, we see that even the adversity in our lives are gifts that help not only help others but ourselves.

Amen.

Day 108

Today's prayer: Lord . . .

Thank You for purpose and meaning. We may not always know our purpose and meaning, but You promised that we would always have it.

Remove those times when we get distracted by the need to know our meaning and propose, and remind us to simply move in faith.

Help us to make "remove and move" the way we walk our faithful path across this life to You.

Remove the doubt and fears and, most important, move us in faith and hope.

Amen.

Day 109

Today's prayer: Lord . . .

There are many prayers being said today, and many more prayers that should be said. These prayers, spoken or unspoken, are cries for help and direction.

We are not alone in needing these answers, but we ask that You make today different. Rather than us looking for answers, let us be the answer to a prayer.

Make us diligent in our search to be an answer to people crying out for help, whether they have prayed or not.

You know who they are.

Show us who they are.

Move us to them.

Make us act in Your love.

Amen.

Day 110

Today's prayer: Lord . . .

So many of us are unintentional hoarders. We may not accumulate physical clutter that weighs down our journeys, but we carry unnecessary emotional and spiritual burdens.

The world would have us believe that these are life lessons and that they are good. True wisdom does not come from our experiences and what happened in our past, but from living with You in this moment. In fact, our past only works to limit the experiences of the present.

Help us to lose our past and tap into You, the source of true wisdom, and to stop living a life less than what You want for us.

Help us to reboot our lives daily and start new, clean, and fresh. Those who come into our lives do not deserve to be burdened by our past mistakes and stupid decisions and the fears that those experiences create. They don't need to carry that baggage to be with us.

We see that this reboot is possible only through our fully realizing what Your forgiveness means. Open our eyes to this wisdom and let that carry us forward into the life You intended.

Amen.

Day 111

Today's prayer: Lord . . .

When we pray, help us to learn to keep our eyes focused on you, rather than the difficulties that caused us to pray.

By Your design, our eyes were built to lead us.

Also, by Your design, your plan is for us to return to You.

Help us to see that it is less important to fully know your plan for us than it is to keep our eyes focused on You.

For is we look to you constantly and for all things, your plan will be revealed in its time.

Amen.

Day 112

Today's prayer: Lord . . .

We often look for signs and wonders as direction for our lives. Sadly, they are rare.

Yet You do lead us and answer our prayers with signs that are common and built into our very nature and being. These often go overlooked.

Help us to see Your direction and guidance in the tears that we cry. They water the seeds of change, the tears of happiness. They lead to more fruits in our acts of love. The tears of pain, suffering, and fear are watering the weeds in our lives that need to be removed.

May the smiles in our lives warm the good fruit of action, just as the sun warms and nourishes a garden. Let the anger we feel till the fields of useless chaff under, so that it no longer chokes those things and people that stand in the way of what You intended to grow from our meager but loving existence.

Help us to listen to You in the common sounds of life, for this is where Your voice resounds the loudest.

Help us to listen.

Amen.

Day 113

Today's prayer: Lord . . .

You told us that You "are with us always, even to the end of time."

What an amazing promise. You are with us on good days. You are with us on days when we are troubled.

Help us to NEVER forget this important aspect of life and to be on constant vigil, looking for Your presence.

Give those who need security and comfort protection at the appropriate time. Give those who hunger fulfillment. Give those who need friends the presence of real love. Give those who have questions the appropriate answers. Give those who hurt comfort.

Give us the ability to be one or more of those important gifts to another today, just as You are to us!

We know that You are with us to the end. Let us be with others in the same way.

Amen.

Day 114

Today's prayer: Lord . . .

Today we ask that You give us broader insight into who You are, even though we already know the answer. . . .

You are love!

You are peace!

You are grace!

You are joy!

You are strength!

You are safety!

You are shelter!

You are power!

You are the Creator!

You are the Comforter!

YOU ARE THE WAY, THE TRUTH, AND THE LIFE!

Keep all of this ever present in our life. Make each the very fabric of our beliefs and actions.

Help us to be constant vessels of these truths, having them in such abundance that they pour out into the world and show others who You are by what we have become. When we are with You, who and what can be against us?

All things will bow to Your name . . .

All loneliness . . .

All sickness . . .

All financial challenges . . .

All fear . . .

All hunger . . .

All sadness . . .

Every woe that we are encountering.

Thank You for allowing us into Your family. Help us to constantly remember what this means.

Amen.

Day 115

Today's prayer: Lord . . .

You rule over time.

You were here yesterday.

You are here today.

And You will be here tomorrow.

You are the immovable rock upon which all things lasting are built. You came to us with more than words of advice; You showed us how to live and act, yet we continue to worry and fret over the little things.

We ask that You strengthen our faith in You so that, like You, we are more than words.

We are action, not to our glory but to Yours.

Amen.

Day 116

Today's prayer: Lord . . .

The scriptures tell us that "the heavens and earth are filled with Your glory." Yet in our hectic pace we often miss seeing You in it and we miss the real experiences and lessons planned for us.

You are there with us not just in the good times but also in the bad times.

Help us to see more of You today so that we experience the wonder and joy that calm our days and confirm that what we are doing is right.

This is more than the "peace that surpasses all understanding." It is peace that drives our purpose and makes You real not only in the world but also in us.

Amen.

Day 117

Today's prayer: Lord . . .

Thank You for Your guidance.

You are always with us, whether we realize it or not.

Help us to realize that obedience is more than going in the right direction. It is walking the path that You have planned for us.

We will get where You planned for us to go.

Today we choose the path. Make it clear and easy, and every footstep one of value.

Amen.

Day 118

Today's prayer: Lord . . .

"Seek First the kingdom of God…"

As I awake each morning, let the first thing that I do is to look to You.

It may be in a simple thought, or a prayer.

Let my day start by looking to You before anything else.

Today, I thank You and ask that you help me to never take your blessings for granted.

For in doing this I place your admonition to "seek first" in the proper place in my life.

Amen.

Day 119

Today's prayer: Lord . . .

You are the Creator.

This world is an amazing work and a wonder to behold. Give us a new appreciation for it today and, from that, move us to do the things that show our gratitude.

Words are empty and hollow. We need not say a thing.

Let us show this world who we are and how grateful we are with our actions, for they truly do speak louder than words.

Amen.

Day 120

Today's prayer: Lord . . .

You once told a wonderful parable of a sower and seeds.

Some seeds fell on a path, others in rocky soil and still others in good soil.

What happened to the plants was directly affected by where they were planted.

This also applies to our prayers.

Help us to pray with discretion.

Make our prayers seeds of bountiful harvests.

Let us not waste our prayers in soil that only ends in wasted energy.

Amen.

Day 121

Today's prayer: Lord . . .

This is a simple prayer.

Hopefully each of us prays many other prayers during our days, asking for as many things as there are grains of sand on the beach.

The interesting thing is that the answer to each prayer has existed since the moment of creation. Even more awe-inspiring is the fact that the answer to each prayer is exactly the same.

Help us to hear that answer, which is, "Trust me, I have given you what you need to get that. Now go do something about it."

Whatever our prayers today, move us to recognize them and then go and do something about them.

Amen.

Day 122

Today's prayer: Lord . . .

All of our prayers ultimately focus on comfort or happiness, for ourselves or others.

There is nothing wrong with these prayers because we are looking to You rather than to the world for answers.

But today our prayer is different. We are not asking for our happiness or that of others.

Today we ask, "Are You happy with us?"

Show us what we can do and make asking this of You a regular part of our day.

Amen.

Day 123

Today's prayer: Lord . . .

You showed us how to live with empathy and compassion. As we walk through life, we are overwhelmed with the pain and needs of others. Sadly, we become callused and insensitive.

We have missed many opportunities to help those who really need it. Many times we were intended to be the only source of help and comfort.

Pour Your spirit upon us and soften our hearts, so that through us You can touch those who need You.

Amen.

Day 124

Today's prayer: Lord . . .

Today we pray for those who need it but would reject praying with us.

Remove their pain, worries and problems.

Replace them with help happiness and peace.

Let them feel that something is different.

Move them to ask "why?"

In that question bring them to a realization that it was you who made the difference in their life.

In this simple and selfless act on our part, others will be brought into the fold., to serve and fulfill your plan.

Amen.

Day 125

Today's prayer: Lord . . .

We are meant to be in the world but not of the world. This seems like a very simple and straightforward piece of advice, but it is much deeper than simple guidance for our behavior.

The world is full of sadness, pain, suffering, sickness, hunger, and injustice. It is not a happy place. There is no reason to desire that which it says we need, yet by our very nature we seek to fit in.

We seek a common language and look to have common experiences. We are told by the world that we are nothing until we have or do or get certain things on its terms. We believe what it tells us and risk it all for the sake of fitting in and obtaining happiness and fulfillment.

Help us to realize that the world's promises of happiness are hollow and that real fulfillment and happiness can only be had on Your terms.

If we are to be happy, that happiness is found in the language of love.

If the experiences are to be common, may they be acts of altruism, full of selfless kindness, caring, and sharing.

Let not our hearts be lured into believing that happiness is around the corner, for that will never appear. It already resides within us.

We claim it now and begin sharing this wonderful gift, against the better judgment of the world because we are in it and not of it. We are Yours.

Amen.

Day 126

Today's prayer: Lord . . .

Thank You for another day and the opportunities that this day affords.

For some it's a time to rest and heal . . .

For others a time to work . . .

For others a time to play . . .

And for others a time to move closer to closure.

Whatever the case, let Your light shine in us and through us. Let each day carry a simple message of love. Protect us from the enemy, no matter what our needs are and what challenges lie ahead.

It's a new day and a wonderful gift.

Thank You. Enjoy it along with us.

Amen.

Day 127

Today's prayer: Lord ...

This world is full of miracles, things that happen. But we fail to see because we have grown comfortable in their presence, we think we understand their presence, or we lack understanding and cannot see them at all.

The lack of the miraculous in our lives is not Your fault but ours, for miracles abound.

Restore in us the childlike awe of life so that we see more often the wonders around us, and through these miracles we see Your miraculous presence in not only this world but our lives as well. Of all the miracles in this world, we need to see that it is us. You are the greatest and are here with one specific purpose.

We are miracles.

THANK YOU!

Let us recognize and live like we are.

Amen.

Day 128

Today's prayer: Lord . . .

Thank You for being our strength. With You on our side, nothing can be against us.

The true blessings in this world do not come from our efforts but from You working through us.

Herein lies our prayer. . . .

We are praying not for strength to overcome, for there will always be something stronger, but for the ability to submit to You so that Your omnipotence and glory enter this world through us.

Lord, give us the strength to be weak.

Amen.

Day 129

Today's prayer: Lord . . .

Inspire us today in ways that we have never before been inspired.

Move us to accomplish great and wonderful things. With You all things are possible.

It is our weakness that stands in the way of the strength of Your love's entry into this world and to those who need it. Change that in us so that others' lives may be changed through us.

Amen.

Day 130

Today's prayer: Lord . . .

Help us to remember that we will never find the devil in a graveyard.

We wrongly believe that when we are on the right path, it will be easy. That couldn't be further from the truth. The more life we exude, the greater the attacks and the greater the need for Your protection and strength.

You never promised that our lives would be easy; You did, however, promise that they would be worth it.

Help us to not only overcome our obstacles but to make them perfectly align with Your purpose and mission for each of us.

Amen.

Day 131

Today's prayer: Lord . . .

Your messages to us are simple, and we make them more complicated than You meant.

You told us to let our light shine, but this world surrounds us with darkness.

Let our lights be beacons of hope, caring, honesty, respect, selflessness, giving, loyalty, and devotion. The world so badly needs this light, and we are those lights.

Make it possible for us to shine brightly.

We pray for that opportunity today.

Let us not miss that chance.

Amen.

Day 132

Today's prayer: Lord . . .

Use my struggles to help others.

Use me and my accomplishments to inspire others to continue their walk.

My struggles are not unique to me. Others are going through the same.

Give me the answers to my problems so that I can share them with others and lead them out.

Not to my glory but to Yours.

Not for my benefit, but to theirs.

Amen.

Day 133

Today's prayer: Lord . . .

We pray for many reasons. Whatever those reasons, help us to realize that we are more than just a person who prays.

We are often the answer to prayers.

Spark the fire in us that moves us from mere praying to being an example of Your love and the answer to prayers—ours and those of others.

Amen.

Days 134

Today's prayer: Lord . . .

We work diligently to be content with the present and with our current gifts and blessings. Yet each of us has been given fears, dreams, hungers, desires, and aspirations that distract us from the present.

These are also gifts and part of the way You created us. Give us a better understanding of how those gifts fit into today and were given to us to keep us from complacency, and to drive us to become more like what You want us to be.

Do not allow us to become comfortable with today, for we will truly stop living abundantly and walk among the living dead if we do so.

Amen.

Day 135

Today's prayer: Lord . . .

Inspire us today.

Make our passion and actions intense and unstoppable.

Take us in the directions that only serve Your purpose.

As this happens, our worries and concerns will disappear and we will see that they are really meaningless. We will then realize that our cups truly do run over with Your goodness, kindness, and mercy—those things that need to spill out and touch the lives of others.

This all starts with inspiration "in spirit," the spark that gives us life and turns into words and actions that affect the lives of others.

Inspire us, dear Lord.

Amen.

Day 136

Today's prayer: Lord . . .

What do I say when I don't have the words?

Inspire my prayers in ways unimaginable.

You know my heart and my real needs.

You know what tomorrow holds and You have gone to prepare a place for me in it.

Rather than me searching my heart for the right words, I ask that You search my heart and answer its needs,

I will simply rest in You and know that You are God!

Help me to see that oftentimes we simply need to "be still!"

Amen.

Day 137

Today's prayer: Lord . . .

How often have we heard someone ask, "Can you spare some change?"

Although that person is asking for money, there is a deeper meaning hidden within that question. The person may be hungry but want the pains in his or her stomach to change into satisfaction.

The person may be craving drugs or alcohol and want that desire to change into fulfillment. Still others may want the cries of their children to change to laughter. "Change," to them, is a small gift. The change they really want is more meaningful.

Help us to recognize that all types of change are gifts, and that everyone actually desires these gifts in some way. For without "change," our pains, hungers, and desires will remain. Change is required to turn our cries into laughter.

We, dear Lord, are no different from those who humbly stand on the corner hoping that someone will help them with some change.

And today we humbly ask You, "Can You help us with some change?"

Amen.

Day 138

Today's prayer: Lord . . .

Your love is constant. Thank You. Yet there are days when You feel so close and days when You feel far away.

We know that there is a reason for all things, and how we act must be controlled by our internal commitment and resolve— and not by the world around us.

Make the love in us more like Your love from today forward, growing yet constant and unwavering so that, like You, we become a small but dependable light of hope to those who need it.

Amen.

Day 139

Today's prayer: Lord . . . .

Thank You for the morning and all that the day ahead holds.

Help us to remember that if we keep our eyes on You and constantly look to You for guidance and act in love, we will end the day knowing peace and contentment.

Be with us today, helping us to feel Your presence in ways we have never felt before, sparking acts that awe and amaze the world around us—not for our glory but for Yours.

Amen.

Day 140

Today's prayer: Lord . . .

Thank You for love and for loving us. We easily recognize what a wonderful gift love is, yet we fail to see the burden that it carries.

You long to hear us say those three simple words to You, for all You have given us. Once we speak them, You take the entire responsibility to guard and protect the one who spoke those words.

Help us to speak those words not lightly or selfishly but with gratitude, knowing the burden that it carries to the recipient.

We love You.

Amen.

Day 141

Today's prayer: Lord . . .

You advised that we live in this world, but are not to be of it.

The world around us is constantly luring us with the need for more and better things. Fill us with the contentment that leads our frail spirits with peace.

Help us to know that what we have is enough and that Your promise to take care of our every need is real so that we can walk through this life in true gratitude.

Amen.

Day 142

Today's prayer: Lord . . .

Every day we are afforded chances.

We have chances to be loud, aggressive, hostile and demeaning.

Or

We have chances to be quiet, loving, forgiving and caring.

We are given chances to be of this world.

Or

We are given chances to be Your child.

Help us to choose wisely!

Amen.

Day 143

Today's prayer: Lord ...

We pray for blessings and we also pray to be blessings.

We often do not realize what we are praying for.

Blessings do not come without a cost.

Help us to remember that blessing require discipline and chastisement.

Help us to remember that blessings require trust, fear and obedience.

Help us to see that blessings require temptation, suffering and forgiveness.

Blessings may come with a cost and they also have a benefit.

For those who pay the price, they also receive delight, strength, purity and endurance.

We know the cost and will continue to ask you to bless us, for there is nothing better than being one of your blessed children. For it is in those blessing that our "cups overflow" and we can bless others.

Amen.

Day 144

Today's prayer: Lord . . .

Heaven and earth sing to Your glory continuously. Life itself is an amazing song, perfect in all ways.

Open our eyes to that fact that the world is more than a chorus; it is also our teacher.

There are days that are clear and bright, and our path is easy to see and travel, and the songs are easy to sing. Other days are cloudy and our walk is dim and unclear, and the song is harder to hear.

Help us to learn to walk forward in faith regardless of our view and to continuously sing Your glory with more than our voices.

Let our song and Your glory show in our thoughts, words, and actions so that we join and are always with heaven and earth in singing the song that matters.

Amen.

Day 145

Today's prayer: Lord . . .

We desire our lives to be different and better, yet we refuse to change the things that got us here.

Help us to realize that we are where we are because of who we are, and our current state of being will not change until we change those things that define us: our habits, our desires, and our repeated behaviors.

In truth, change will only happen when we realize that we are who we are because of who You are.

Help us to make that fact part of our deepest desire, and give us the desire to become more and more like You and less and less like ourselves. Just like John the Baptist each and every day we will grow closer to what You planned and meant for us to be.

Amen.

Day 146

Today's prayer: Lord . . .

Sadly, there are many people in many of Your children's lives that are toxic.

The reasons that they are in their lives are many.

It doesn't matter what the reason is, if their presence hurts Your child,

Change those toxic individuals or remove them from Your child's lives so that Your child can walk freely.

Give Your children discernment so they see who these people are and give them the strength to let them go and not look back.

Separate the proverbial good seed from the chaff so that these children live in peace and better serve You.

Amen.

Day 147

Today's prayer: Lord . . .

Your ways make the ways of this world look foolish. Contrary to what many believe, wisdom is not the result of learning and the accumulation of more information but from experiencing life and the ability to narrow our perspectives to what is important.

The same holds true with success and abundance. The world would have us believe that this is the accumulation of worldly possessions and a fulfillment of our desires. The truth is that our success comes from a recognition that everything we have and do is a gift, and the constant use of these gifts is to the benefit of our call.

Our gifts are precious, but unlike what the world does, we do not lock them away. We use them.

Help us to make more and more of what we do and say each day.

Show others the folly and foolishness of the world.

Change the lives of others through the way we live our lives.

Amen.

Day 148

Today's prayer: Lord . . .

If I am wrong, right me!

If I am lost, guide me!

If I begin to give up, keep me going!

As You led Israel through the desert, be my light in dark times and the pillar by day.

I turn my entire life over to You. I trust in You fully and will walk in faith.

Amen.

Day 149

Today's prayer: Lord . . .

We long to hear Your voice, yet we neglect to realize that we hear it continuously and often miss Your messages.

You talk to us in the majesty of the sunrises, in the laughter of children, in gentle rains and violent storms, in calm and peaceful waters, through friends and enemies, through the songs we hear and the words we read, and, most of all, through all of life itself.

Help us to listen and hear Your voice, and let us join in with the other voices and carry Your messages to those who have yet to hear them.

Amen.

Day 150

Today's prayer: Lord . . .

There are no other Gods before You .

You are the King of Kings.

You are the Lord of Lords.

You are the Master of Masters.

We are easily deceived into allowing "gods" into our life and letting them control us. The deception is real, and it can easily erode our being until we are controlled by a god other than You.

Protect me, dear Lord. Search my heart and open my eyes to anything or anyone that may be ruling over a subtle part of my life.

Give me the strength to resist and overcome, so that I may grow and bring more glory and praise to Your name.

Amen.

Day 151

Today's prayer: Lord . . .

My faith is in the unseen. I have no need for images or idols to believe in You.

Burn into my heart that I am Yours by my faith and not because of anything I have done, and that by my faith in the unseen, my thoughts, words, and deeds are now used to Your glory and perfect plan.

Create in me a clean heart and renew a righteous spirit within me.

Restore unto me the joy of salvation so that I may act totally in gratitude and thanksgiving for this wonderful blessing, living in a way that brings others to You . . .

To Your GLORY and PRAISE!

Amen.

Day 152

Today's prayer: Lord . . .

I will not take Your name in vain. Some believe that this means simply using it as a curse word, but I know that it goes beyond swearing. It means using Your name and our relationship as a curse word.

I will not call upon You to curse or hurt another for any reason. Judgment and retribution are Yours and Yours alone.

I do not know the reasons for other's behaviors, and I accept that everything that happens to me is part of Your perfect plan.

Guard my thoughts and emotions.

Put anger and hurt in their place so that my every thought, word, and deed is to Your glory and praise.

Amen.

Day 153

Today's prayer: Lord . . .

On the seventh day You rested and looked at Your creation, and You saw that it, like You, was good, true, and beautiful.

You asked us to do the same. Help us to set aside time to make all of our days special and holy.

We should not set aside a single day to do so; we should "rest in You and Your love" every day!

Help us to remember to stop and rest in You daily, and to see that what You have done for us, and around us, is also good, true, and beautiful.

In doing so, we will live and breathe gratitude for what You have done, and our praise will sing from the highest mountains.

Amen.

Day 154

Today's prayer: Lord . . .

Make my life an honor to my earthly parents, and make my life an honor to You, my heavenly parent.

Guide my every thought, word, and action so that they never disgrace others or You.

The world would have us believe that there are deep-seated reasons for what we do. Many blame their failures on the "sins of our father and mothers."

There is nothing further from the truth. My failures are mine and mine alone.

My success is entirely because of You. Help me to see what You see: I am made good through Your intervention and forgiveness, and through those gifts I live as an honor to my name, my parents, and especially to You.

Amen.

Day 155

Today's prayer: Lord . . .

Remove from me any thought of harm for another. Let my every action be a direct reflection of what is on my inside.

You told us that any angry thought directed at another makes us guilty of murder. Worse yet is the fact that angry and vengeful thoughts are like taking poison and expecting the other person to die.

Guard my words and actions so that they never go against Your will.

Go beyond this and guide my thoughts so that the soil from which my actions grow is clean and pure.

I ask this in Your name. I ask You to pray for me.

I ask that this be done for the glory of God so that He is praised and others come closer to Him.

Amen.

Day 156

Today's prayer: Lord . . .

Long ago You told us to avoid adultery. In other words, You said stay ever faithful to those people important to You. Although the message was specifically interpreted and limited to our earthly relationships, the hidden meaning sent is much bigger.

Help me to see what You intend me to be perfectly faithful to . . . especially You!

Let me never become unfaithful to You or anything that is part of Your plan for me, for in my faithfulness to You and Your plan, Your glory will be shown and others will be brought into Your presence.

Amen.

Day 157

Today's prayer: Lord . . .

Burned into my heart is something You told Your people long ago:

"Do not take that which is not yours."

Help me to see that this goes beyond the physical things around me and includes other people's time, their feelings and emotions, their help and support—in fact, anything that is not mine.

Help me to see that the things I have are more than sufficient for me to fulfill Your plan for me.

If I need more, show me how to obtain them without expecting them for nothing, for Your plan for me is my work for You!

Let all of my work always give glory to You, and in doing so I will never take from another for any reason!

Amen.

Day 158

Today's prayer: Lord . . .

"Don't lie."

Could it be any clearer? As I look at and listen to the world around me, I am sickened by how so many people have forgotten this simple command.

Our world is filled with so much falsehood, so many half-truths. Words flow freely from our mouths, and these people believe that these lies have no impact on their hearts.

Nothing could be further from the truth.

Help us to NOT be like those of this world. Let our "yes be yes" and our "no be no." In holding true to our words, we are also holding true to THE WORD.

Your glory can be shown not only through our words but also our actions!

Amen.

Day 159

Today's prayer: Lord . . .

GRATITUDE.

Your life taught me that this is one of the very important stones within the foundation of living the life You intended for me to live. Long ago You told others not to look at those around them and wish that they had those things.

NOT their land and living arrangements . . .

NOT the people in their lives . . .

NOT their possessions . . .

NOT ANYTHING!

What is theirs is theirs.

What is mine is mine.

Being jealous of others is my telling You that You have given me dirt.

How ungrateful!

Forgive me for the times when I was that way.

Let me see that what I have is more than enough.

In fact, "Your grace is enough for me."

Thank You!

I will use the gifts I have to Your glory and to the benefit of those who love You.

Amen.

Day 160

Today's prayer: Lord . . .

The past ten prayers have focused on one of the original Ten Commandments. Even though each of these commandments appears quite easy to follow, as I look deeper into each, I can see that I am not pure and blameless.

When You walked the earth, You told us that You were bringing us a new commandment, that in one way the fulfillment met the criteria of the original ten. In another way it is less self-serving.

That new commandment is LOVE!

The second part of Your new commandment is: "Love your neighbor as yourself."

Help me to realize that anyone and everyone is my neighbor.

Remove any hatred and indifference from my life.

Let the "fulfillment of the law" that You brought into this world become apparent through my life, through my every thought, word, and deed.

Let all that I do . . .

Be done in gratitude . . .

Be done in love . . .

Be done to Your glory . . .

Be done to bring more "neighbors" into Your love.

Amen.

Day 161

Today's prayer: Lord ...

The first and most important part of Your new commandment is: "Love God with all your heart, soul, and mind."

Make this commandment EVER-PRESENT in my being.

Make all that I think, say, and do show my love.

Make all that I think, say and do show Your love.

Make all that I think, say, and do show my gratitude for what You have done for me.

Let me be LOVE, so that Your glory and love are more manifest in this world.

Amen.

Day 162

Today's prayer: Lord . . .

Fill my every thought with those things that are good, true, and beautiful . . .

Actions that are noble, right, pure, lovely, admirable, excellent, and praiseworthy.

It is these thoughts and actions that will water and nourish the seeds of comfort and provide a harvest of peace.

Thank You for these wonderful gifts and for Your guidance to make them meaningful.

Amen.

Day 163

Today's prayer: Lord . . .

I thank You for being patient with me. I often pray for You to open my eyes and ears so that I may better serve You and the world around me, and then I neglect to look and listen. I seek answers but spend so much time talking that I often miss hearing them.

Help me to be a better listener.

Give me the strength to patiently listen.

Give me the peace that helps me understand and the courage to act on the message.

Amen.

Day 164

Today's prayer: Lord . . .

Thank You for knowing my every detail and watching over me.

Thank You for my strengths and weaknesses.

It is reassuring to know that You are with me every step of my life and that You control everything I encounter—every event, every decision I have to make—good or bad.

I am capable of doing the right things. It is amazing that I am capable of enduring everything that comes into my life not because it's easy, but because each of these things is meant to be worth it.

Amen.

Day 165

Today's prayer: Lord . . .

You are both the beginning and the end. Help me to look back to the beginning with simple gratitude and look to the end with anticipation.

Sadness, regret, and remorse only blind me to the wonderful life that You long for me to enjoy.

Help me to remember that the enemies of abundance only come to me through invitation. They are no longer welcome at my "party".

I ask that their places at my table of celebration be occupied by hope, joy, and love—Your greatest gifts!

Amen.

Day 166

Today's prayer: Lord . . .

Timing is everything, and Your timing is perfect, although it may not seem like it. I am in this place and time not because of my mistakes and flaws but as part of Your perfect plan.

Help me to truly believe that promise, that all things work to the glory of those who love You. Move me to act upon that belief.

Today I pray as if it all depends on You (because it does), and I will act as if it all depends on me (because it does)!

True abundance and happiness are at my doorstep if I simply open the door and let them in.

Thank You, thank You, thank You.

I love You, dear Lord.

Amen.

Day 167

Today's prayer: Lord . . .

You are my hero in ways unimaginable.

You taught me that one of my greatest enemies is fear.

You fearlessly walked this earth, but it was not because You didn't taste fear.

You showed me that fearlessness is in direct proportion to my faith.

As a hero You led the way and told me that You were going to prepare a place for us. What do we have to fear?

My hero is already there!

You promised me that I do not need to be afraid. Thank You!

I ask that You do not take my fear away, but instead give me so much faith that there is no room for that fear to attack me.

Amen.

Day 168

Today's prayer: Lord . . .

Help me remember that I am not only called to be *in* Your presence at every moment. But I am also called to *be* Your presence in the very same moment.

Let me never misrepresent who You are, whether in my thoughts, words, or deeds.

Help me remember that lives are often touched and changed by a single word or a small, simple act.

Help me inspire others and change lives through Your inspiration—that is, Your spirit flowing from me.

I will be in Your presence, and through me You are present in the world when You are present in me.

Amen.

Day 169

Today's prayer: Lord . . .

You are not *in* the grand scheme of things; You *are* the grand scheme.

As I consider my part in this cosmic drama, I see that my role may be that of an insignificant "walk-on," made meaningful only by Your presence.

Nothing I can do will help or hinder anything in Your plan. My life can be made more meaningful through following Your direction and standing ever closer to You.

Help me today to be more attentive to Your direction and to "let go and let God."

Amen.

Day 170

Today's prayer: Lord . . .

One of the greatest regrets of mankind is the realization that someone has missed a chance. There are so many things in this world that distract us from living the life You have planned for us.

Help us to see more clearly each day so that we do not miss the greatest gifts we've been given.

In the opportunity to do Your work . . .

In the lessons we learn and, most of all, in the people around us . . .

Help us to never have to live knowing we had the chance but now it's too late.

Amen.

Day 171

Today's prayer: Lord . . .

Let me not forget: My to-do list is so big that I often forget to do the little things that make a huge difference.

Let me not forget: I often am so busy I forget to look for people who need my help and comfort.

Let me not forget: I often neglect to stop and pray for those who need it most.

Let me not forget: I do not look around and count the blessings that I already have.

Let me not forget: Living begins with my gratitude for the blessings around me and grows as those blessings are shared.

Let me not forget what You have done for me, and help me to remember to share Your love with the world around me.

Amen.

Day 172

Today's prayer: Lord . . .

What do we have to gain by praying?

Perhaps, we have more to lose!

Let us pray and lose anger, ego, fear, depression, greed and insecurity.

Help us to see that oftentimes the answer to our prayers is not in what we gain, but in what we lose!

This makes room for those gifts that You have longed to give to us.

The greatest of which is Your Love!

Amen.

Day 173

Today's prayer: Lord . . .

Every story has a beginning and an ending.

Help us to see that every story should begin and end with prayer.

Open our stories with prayers of faith and submission.

Close our stories with prayers of thanksgiving.

When the book of life is opened, let all of the credit go to you!

Amen.

Day 174

Today's prayer: Lord . . .

There is a simple answer to every situation.

It is to "Serenity Pray" it to conclusion.

Remind us of the full prayer rather than just the first part, which goes;

God, give me grace to accept with serenity, the things that cannot be changed,

Courage to change the things, which should be changed,

and the Wisdom to distinguish, the one from the other.

Living one day at a time,

Enjoying one moment at a time,

Accepting hardship as a pathway to peace,

Taking, as Jesus did,

This sinful world as it is,

Not as I would have it,

Trusting that You will make all things right,

If I surrender to Your will,

So that I may be reasonably happy in this life,

And supremely happy with You forever in the next.

Amen.

Amen.

Day 175

Today's prayer: Lord . . .

Millions of people create lists of resolutions, lists of things that they wish to stop doing. Let me not fall prey to this seldom successful endeavor!

Instead help me to create a list of more wonderful things to do in service to You so that the habits I possess will have no room in my life! And each of those things that I want to leave me will be replaced by things that are good, true, and beautiful!

Guide my choices today and every day going forward. In doing so, I will better serve You and help bring others into Your service!

Amen.

Day 176

Today's prayer: Lord . . .

Take control of one problem in my life that is taking the joy of living from me and standing in the way of my ability to serve You.

Make this a daily prayer, until everything in my life that separates me from happiness and You is gone and replaced with overflowing gifts that I can share with others.

Amen.

Day 177

Today's prayer: Lord . . .

Every minute is a precious gift. Help me order my life so that not one minute is wasted. Help me to use each minute to fulfill Your purpose in this world, leaving each moment better for my having been in it.

I can try to do it alone, but I ask that You come into "my minutes" and leave them better for Your having been in them also.

It is when we share our moments with You that we can fully experience the abundance that You have promised.

Whether at work or play or rest, make each moment better than I could ever imagine by Your presence and with Your presence.

Amen.

Day 178

Today's prayer: Lord . . .

As I greet the morning, let my heart be filled with excitement and hope.

Let these feelings drive my every action and interaction.

I will look for the moments to show Your love.

Guide me to these moments. I do not need to travel or roam to find my purpose. Everything I need is here, within and around me.

Remove the distractions and focus my life on things good, true, and beautiful, using me to change my life and the lives of others.

Amen.

Day 179

Today's prayer: Lord . . .

If there is one thing that I should seek, it is to walk through my life with the same purpose and intensity You did while You were here with us.

Give me the spirit to do the same through the darkest times of despair and the most jubilant of times.

Let me walk like You did.

You came with specific purpose and fulfilled it.

I am here for a specific purpose.

Help me to, like You, fulfill mine.

Amen.

Day 180

Today's prayer: Lord . . .

We all dream of happily ever after, and that is in fact what You want for us. Yet each day we often feel lacking and that there is always something more.

Our "happily ever afters" can be "happily today" if we begin each day with gratitude, not just for the good things in our lives but for everything, past and present.

Help us to realize that our complete past has been a complete blessing that has made us exactly what we are today.

Remove regret and remorse and replace them with gratitude.

Once we have this wonderful new perspective, drive our every action so that our gratitude shows.

If we are truly grateful, we will act like it, and then we will see that our happily ever after is happily today.

Amen.

Day 181

Today's prayer: Lord . . .

In what we call the "Sermon on the Mount," You told us to "seek first the kingdom of God and His righteousness and all things will be added."

How simple that message is, yet it is so misinterpreted. Many are misguided into believing that we will get what we want if we come to You, when the fact of the matter is that we will get what we truly need through our love and service of God.

Believing that we will get our desires fulfilled is very selfish and a sign that we have not yet found a righteous faith. Give me time today to search my heart and ask, "Is today enough?"

Let me reflect on the difference between my real needs, which help me serve You better, and my wants, many of which serve me and not You.

Help me realize that in all things, Your grace and love are enough and totally unwarranted. I deserve and have earned nothing. My only answer to that first question is: "My need is to better serve God."

What matters is in Your plan for me for today. My past and future do not matter. God's grace is what I need.

Amen.

Day 182

Today's prayer: Lord . . .

I often pray to have eyes to see and ears to hear more clearly.

I am also inundated with sights and sounds. I sometimes don't realize that I don't need more; I need less. I am distracted by quantity and do not look for purity and quality of experience. I use the "noise of life" to distract myself from reality.

Today I pray to be blinded and deafened to those things around me that keep me from seeing the truth.

Along with this, give me the strength to accept reality and face the truth with You. Narrow my sight and limit my hearing to only that which serves You so that I am no longer distracted or tempted to stray.

Amen.

Day 183

Today's prayer: Lord . . .

With You for us, who can be against us?

I know this but do not always live it. My life is not lived free from anxiety or insecurity.

I know that You love me, and in that love I am secure.

I need to remember that any fear, anxiety, or insecurity are not from You but are brought into my life by me and my actions.

Free me from myself, for with You even my greatest enemy, myself, cannot work against me.

Amen.

Day 184

Today's prayer: Lord . . .

Many of us were told fairy tales and read stories as children. Many of these stories began with "once upon a time" and ended with "and they lived happily ever after."

I learned that my life is a story, and I am moving through it. I live in the hope that I get to the place where I live "happily ever after." On Your last day here, You promised that You were leaving to prepare a place for me, a place where "happily ever afters" will happen.

Thank You.

Help me to realize that my life does not have to be like a fairy tale. With You all things are possible.

Make my stories go like this: "Once upon a time there was this person. One day he looked at his life and said, 'I am living happily ever after!' And he did!"

You are the author of my life. Write the words of love and encouragement in my heart that let today be the start of my seeing that I am indeed living "happily ever afters" today.

Amen.

Day 185

Today's prayer: Lord . . .

You are the fulfillment of a promise past, and You live as a promise for today. You are our promised future. You came so we could live and have life abundantly.

We thank You.

We often seek the wrong abundance. Help us to find the true abundance that You want for us—abundance in love, abundance in caring, and abundance in the giving of ourselves.

Make it possible for us to give these gifts more often and fully, not from our needs or from our possessions but from the abundance of our hearts.

Help us to realize that all these things are already with us. We just need to see them and accept them as the wonderful gifts that You intended.

Amen.

Day 186

Today's prayer: Lord . . .

Of all the things that You gave to me, the greatest gift is love. Although many will deny it, everyone is built to love.

As with everyone else, in my way I seek to love and to be loved and to fulfill those needs. Many often settle for that which is not real. They will selfishly and desperately seek any form of love to fill that hunger. I pray with gratitude for those who have real love, and I pray for those who lack love.

Help me to recognize the source of this powerful gift fully and to never lose this realization, for all things will pass away but love stands eternal.

I pray that I stand eternally with You, with legs of LOVE.

Amen.

Day 187

Today's prayer: Lord . . .

Each and every day, great things are waiting to happen. When You walked this earth, great and mighty things happened. Although not physically, You still walk this earth . . .

Through us . . .

Through our thoughts . . .

Through our words and through our actions.

Help us to see that through You and through us, great and mighty things can still happen. Make each of us a vessel through which the power of love flows and becomes evident in this world.

Yesterday, today, and tomorrow will be no different without a change. Let us be the first to change, and let our lives be the source of Your great and loving presence in this world.

Amen.

Day 188

Today's prayer: Lord . . .

Remove the worries of those who fear.

Although it may seem like it,

Help them to remember that You are not blind to their tears.

Help them to remember that You are deaf to their cries.

Help them to remember that you are not silent to their pain.

Work in their heart and make it feel that You see. Hear and delivers.

Amen.

Day 189

Today's prayer: Lord . . .

I pray for Your help. I pray for Your blessings.

My prayers are focused on what I can get rather than what I need to do to make a difference in others' lives.

Today I ask that You make me a true prayer warrior.

Give me the strength and means to help others and the motivation to do it.

Make me a blessing to others and move me to be that blessing without expectation of return.

Direct my vision and action outward so that I act in ways that make a difference in this world and the lives of those who matter most to You.

Amen.

Day 190

Today's prayer: Lord . . .

Today I thank You for the people You have brought into my life, those good and bad.

In truth, I have learned something from each, and they have made me who I am.

Be with them today. Make it possible for those who need me to take that step to open the door so that I can be a blessing to them as You are to me.

Amen.

Day 191

Today's prayer: Lord . . .

You have made me with a single purpose: to love. Everyone is made to love and be loved, each in our own way.

You commanded us to love one another, to love our neighbors, to love our brothers and sisters, to love our enemies, to love our parents, and most of all to love You.

The fulfillment of all that You want is through love. Help me to fulfill my purpose with my unique skills and talents, for love now enters the world through me and I see that You are that love.

You are love!

Amen.

Day 192

Today's prayer: Lord . . .

At the lowest point in my life, You became my only hope.

In my darkest times You shined Your light brightly.

At my weakest You became my greatest strength.

In the saddest times You became my only and greatest comfort.

I see You in these times, yet I avoid them with my entire being.

Help me to find hope, light, strength, comfort, and love in good times too! Make it such that I do not need the woes of the world, which makes it easier to see the gifts.

Help me to see that these wonderful things are always present in my life.

Amen.

Day 193

Today's prayer: Lord . . .

When will people realize that we don't have the last word?

You are the alpha and omega—the beginning and the end—and as I ponder this thought, You are also everything in between.

Yet I tend to complicate life by adding my words to Your perfect story. You have said, "Great things can happen," and then I am compelled to add, "for those who wait."

I ignore the fact that it was already a complete sentence.

Take away my desire to add to Your already perfect story and let me simply live in the role and the moment I've been given.

There is much more in the "now" than I realize. I no longer need to add words for the sake of comfort or a feeble excuse for future failure or a buffer for disappointment.

Your first and last words are more than enough, as is everything in between.

Amen.

Day 194

Today's prayer: Lord . . .

The world around me is constantly handing me beauty, and more often than not I miss it. Even worse, many times people are destroying the marvelous gifts from the world.

Help me to never take these natural gifts for granted.

Show me how to treat every moment with true gratitude.
Help me to protect each moment for the beauty it holds, and give me the power to leave it better for my being allowed to be part of it.

Amen.

Day 195

Today's prayer: Lord . . .

At the end of my life, I will ask myself, "Was it enough?" But enough of what?

Give me the clarity to find the life that I want to live and, once I find it, the courage to live it.

Help me to love enough and laugh enough, heal and comfort enough, as long as I live with Your grace and guidance.

Enough is enough! Everyone is called to different lives. None is better or worse than another.

Let me not worry about the quantity of my life but the quality of my life lived. Then it's more than enough.

Amen.

Day 196

Today's prayer: Lord . . .

There are days that hurt. There are days when I have had enough. There are days when I feel totally alone. There are days when the nights are long, dark, and lonely. There are days when I just want to give up.

These are the days I need to be reminded that I am not alone and that You are with me.

Today I pray: Let those who need it hear Your voice lovingly prodding them along with "Please hold on. Everybody hurts."

And let those of us who are not struggling with pain, loneliness, and despair be with those who need someone, for Your voice no longer projects from Your mouth but from ours. Help me to carry that message, "Please hold on. everybody hurts," with more than words. I need to add, "What can I do to help?"

Then allow me to do what is needed to help and heal another of Your dear children.

Amen.

Day 197

Today's prayer: Lord . . .

"And they lived, happily ever after."

Thank You for putting this line in each of our life stories. Help us to realize today that this phrase does not mean the end of the story but from this moment forward. Our waiting is delaying the happiness that is meant for us. Yesterday was not fully happy, and tomorrow's promises are empty.

Happiness is a condition of today; it is a recognition and enjoyment of the people around us, what we have, and the full use of those gifts.

Most of all, fill us with true gratitude, for this is the solid rock that "happily ever after" is built upon.

Amen.

Day 198

Today's prayer: Lord . . .

Help us to remember not to treat prayer as a spare wheel.

We often only pray when our lives go flat.

Help us to look to often during our days.

Remind us that prayer is a wheel, a steering wheel.

Let our prayers steer us in the direction of abundance and authentic happiness.

All to your glory.

Amen.

Day 199

Today's prayer: Lord . . .

"We believe" is more than a statement of our thoughts; it is a declaration of our actions. What we do is controlled by what we believe.

The greatest messages are sent out into this world not by what we write or say but by what we do.

Make our messages scream of our love for You and for this world through acts of kindness and caring, and most of all through our love. For it is through love that You manifest in this world.

And if You are to be here, may it be through us.

Amen.

Day 200

Today's prayer: Lord . . .

Prayer is such a simple, yet multipurpose, gift. We can talk to You about anything. It is sad that everyone does not pray.

Today we pray for all those who need to pray but do not. We pray for those who are sick and suffering so that they are comforted. We pray for the hungry so that they can be fed. We pray for the sad so that they are consoled. We pray for the angry and hurt so that they may find peace.

This prayer could go on almost forever, but we ask that You touch our hearts and bring the words to us that fashion a prayer that makes a difference in this world.

Amen.

Day 201

Today's prayer: Lord . . .

Another day! Thank You!

Each day is filled with triumph and failure, elation and heartbreak. Dreams are created and hopes are dashed.

That is life, and as we go through this life we are callused and hardened to the wonder around us. It is inevitable that, if left alone, we will become cynical.

But we are not alone. You came to turn all things into good things. It is the negative side of our experiences that chains us and keeps us from experiencing the gifts You have put before us.

"Unless you become as little children . . ."

You told us to remove "the shells of cynical adulthood" that we have grown. Soften our hearts. Help us to see that we are ready for amazing things through You and with Your loving care.

Help us to be like children and to return to innocence.

Amen.

Day 202

Today's prayer: Lord . . .

Today we begin a new life, casting off all of the anchors that hampered our journey, shedding the skin of mediocrity, and arising a new creature.

Help us to realize that this is not a onetime event but an ongoing daily process.

Make us a new creature, just as You planned for today, fully prepared to meet the challenges, bringing life to a dying world, and shining beyond anything that this world has to offer.

Amen.

Day 203

Today's prayer: Lord . . .

You rule over all time. You are the beginning and the end. All of our days are both beginnings and ends. A time to cast off the failures of the past, close doors, and move forward unburdened. A time of new beginnings and a time to harvest the fruits of our labor.

It's amazing—we live in a time of times, and each time has its place in Your plan for us. Help us to use our time as You intended that we do.

There is a time and place for all things in our lives. Guide us in doing what is right, for even the time we have is Yours and it must be returned. Let it be well used and fully tested.

Amen.

Day 204

Today's prayer: Lord . . .

Our journey can be represented with a simple symbol: "?"

Along our road there will be many questions. As we meditate on this, there is a difference between looking for the right answers and looking for answers we want to hear are right.

Finding the right answers is not a matter of finding peace in our hearts and fulfilling our desires, for our hearts, minds, and desires are not pure and will mislead us over and over. "Right" is a matter of Your will, which is perfect.

Help us to see that we are often deceived. Not only does the world around us deceive us, but our greatest enemy is ourselves.

Open our eyes to the real answers. This comes through the eyes of others and through Your word and inspiration.

Give us the clarity that comes from our trust in You and not from our own understanding.

Thank You.

Amen.

Day 205

Today's prayer: Lord . . .

You are amazing. Even the smallest part of You is far beyond our comprehension. You are above and beyond this menial existence.

Yet it is Your love and caring that continue to drive You to find ways into this ordinary world and to be with those in need. What we often forget is that You only enter the world through us.

This is a major responsibility and an honor.

Today let us not forget that we are called to bring the extraordinary into this ordinary world.

Help us to look for ways to lift the world up a little closer to heaven and to You to make the simply mundane simply amazing—not for us or our glory but to bring You into more of this world, which desperately needs You.

Amen.

Day 206

Today's prayer: Lord . . .

When You walked this earth, a simple touch healed sickness and brought life to those who died. People flocked to You to get that touch because of their needs.

Things haven't changed. Reach out to us today. Touch us and heal us.

Remove the pain that plagues some of Your children. Remove the fevers of others. Remove the bad experiences, the failures, the guilt, and the remorse.

Free these gentle spirits from their burdens so that they may live and better live the life they, and You, desire.

Amen.

Day 207

Today's prayer: Lord . . .

You have given us so much—so much, in fact, that we take most of it for granted. We receive some things in such measure that we don't see them for the wonderful blessings they are. What we have has made us who we are, and it is who You want us to be.

Thank You.

Help us to realize that we are enough for today.

Help us to use what we have to make the most of today and set the stage for an even better tomorrow.

Keep us moving through this journey toward ever better days, not stopping with remorse or regret and slowing our progress but using these gifts to save the world—at least the part that matters.

Amen.

Day 208

Today's prayer: Lord . . .

You are the truth, and as we reflect on what You have taught us, it stands in direct contradiction to the ways of this world.

We are blessed through our blessing of others. We receive by giving. We become fulfilled through our emptying of ourselves. We learn to live by dying to ourselves.

Thank You for this irony and the wonderful gifts that it brings.

It is only through our faith (another gift) that these truths can be made real in our lives.

We pray that our faith is strengthened and grows so that we may better stand as You did, contrary to this world's ways and to the glory of our Father.

Amen.

Day 209

Today's prayer: Lord . . .

Thank You for putting real purpose and meaning into our lives. It is easy for us to get enticed and distracted by all of the things going on in this world, and to be so busy that we lose the real gems given to us.

Focus our minds and hearts so that we only do that which serves You and the mission that You planned for us from the very beginning of time.

The greatest gifts are those that are most easily overlooked.

Open our eyes and let us live each moment to Your glory and purpose.

Amen.

Day 210

Today's prayer: Lord . . .

Oddly, true victory in this world comes through surrender—
surrender to You. It is not a surrender in the world's sense but of
our will and needs.

In our doing so, the battles that we are fighting will cease
and our most vicious enemies of doubt, fear, worry, and fatigue
retreat.

Make our surrenders complete and binding so that we can
live in victory, not to our glory but to Yours.

Amen.

Day 211

Today's prayer: Lord . . .

You have been called "living water" and the "bread of life." Water and food, two of our most basic needs and most powerful drives—we cannot live without those things.

Help us to thirst and hunger for spiritual sustenance as we do for the world's food and water, for we cannot truly live without You.

Help us to remember that You and only You are the source of it all, and bring to our hearts and minds constant gratitude for these gifts so that whenever we eat or drink—our most basic but sacred event—we remember You as we asked.

Amen.

Day 212

Today's prayer: Lord . . .

Just like You, the time that we have on this earth is limited. You saw that and lived that truth. We often forget and act as if nothing matters.

The truth is, we have but one chance to do it right. There are no second chances or second impressions.

Help us to live as You lived. with an intense sense of purpose, doing what is right and being led fully by You. With You as our guide, there is no failure, only victory and good, lasting impressions that make a difference in our lives and those of others . . . just like You.

Amen.

Day 213

Today's prayer: Lord . . .

I am simply flesh and bones. I deserve nothing, yet You treat me as something special. Thank You.

From my beginning to the end, everything in my life is a gift. You owe me nothing. I am entitled to nothing; I deserve nothing.

There is no righteous reason for me to be selfish, jealous, or guilty. I should only be grateful.

Make my days full of gratitude and fill my heart with the gifts of joy and cheerfulness. Take it to overflowing so that it shows in my every action and Your glory becomes more evident in this world.

Amen.

Day 214

Today's prayer: Lord . . .

My life often becomes so hectic and demanding that I forget to stop and reflect on my nature and intent.

Today I take but a moment to do so and ask Your forgiveness for my failures—for what I have done and for what I have left undone.

I cannot grow without the realization of the wrongs I have done and do so with a truly contrite heart.

Help me to make introspection a regular part of my day and to realize that Your forgiveness and even my forgiveness of myself is a gift, and a promise of a better tomorrow.

Thank You.

Amen.

Day 215

Today's prayer: Lord . . .

It is said that a person would climb the highest mountain to be with the one he loves. We often forget about the hill You climbed for us because of Your love.

Thank You.

It is said that a person would swim the deepest sea to be with the one he loves. We forget You walked on water to show us Your love.

Thank You.

No greater gift can we give than our life for the one we love.

Thank You.

Help us remember these priceless gifts, and spark in us the passion to go beyond simple and meaningless words of thanks to sincere acts of gratitude.

Amen.

Day 216

Today's prayer: Lord . . .

You desire that we live not a sullen life but one that experiences the joy of living every step of the way.

The world would have us living such that no one would want what we have. The truth is that we are meant to live life fully and abundantly. We are here to live such that others open the door to You because of what they see You've done for us.

Guide our actions. Keep us safe and happy. Let us be Your beacon of hope and fulfillment to a world that so badly needs it for Your glory.

Thank You for this opportunity.

Amen.

Day 217

Today's prayer: Lord . . .

You are able to do measurably more than I ask and even more than I could ever imagine.

May Your will make Your presence real in my life and in this world.

Make the unimaginable happen so that Your glory is undeniably real in our lives and in this world, not just today but every day.

Amen.

Day 218

Today's prayer: Lord . . .

Blanket us.

Cover our thoughts, words, and deeds.

Cover our wants and our needs.

Blanket us.

Give us the warmth of Your spirit. Fire up our souls so that we move to spread Your love.

Blanket us.

Cover us with Your grace and forgiveness, and open our hearts to the gratitude that we need to show. From under this blanket our world will see Your comfort, peace, and glory in a way that they could not with their eyes uncovered.

Amen.

Day 219

Today's prayer: Lord . . .

Open our eyes to our blessings.

So often we recognize the gift in the moment and take it for granted in the next. Other times we are so focused on those things that we don't have that we miss what You have given us, making ourselves feel totally empty.

Help us to continuously recognize that what we have and what we don't have are both blessings. Help us to be deeply grateful for both, for it is all a blessing. More important, they are on loan and will soon be returned.

Amen.

Day 220

Today's prayer: Lord . . .

We simply want to say thank You.

Each of us has many things to be grateful for.

Bring to mind those things for which we should be grateful during the course of the day so that we learn to live in continuous gratitude for Your love and gifts.

Amen.

Day 221

Today's prayer: Lord . . .

Today is special, not because something great happened in the past or because we have planned something amazing. It is special because it is a day made by You.

Any day in which we feel Your presence is fulfilled and worthy of a celebration in our hearts.

Join in our todays.

Make them special with Your presence so that we can say, "This is the day the Lord has made. Let us be glad and rejoice."

Amen.

Day 222

Today's prayer: Lord . . .

We have an old saying that "when one door closes, another one opens." That is true sometimes; there are times in our lives when You close doors to simplify our lives and other times to protect us.

That is because You know our needs better than we do.

Help us to focus on those open doors that You want us to pursue, forget about the doors that close, and ignore those things that take us further from Your plan for us.

Amen.

Day 223

Today's prayer: Lord . . .

We live in a world of discontentment. We never seem to have enough or what we think we need.

Forgive us for thinking that we are smarter than You and that we know our needs better than You do. We are not God. You told us to be content with what we have.

Today is all we have, and that is more than enough.

Coveting what others have is not only childish and immature, but it is a sin that separates us from fully experiencing Your love.

Change this in us today.

Amen.

Day 224

Today's prayer: Lord . . .

Our lives are in Your hands. We say that often but don't realize what we've committed to.

We do it as a last resort in frustration, not realizing that when we ask in true faith and obedience, You are our first and last resort.

Help us to do this and listen to Your guidance so that our lives shine to Your glory.

Let our lives be fulfilled and working as a beacon of Your love.

Amen.

Day 225

Today's prayer: Lord . . .

You promised that we would live in abundance and happiness, and we are often misdirected and misinterpreted by our worldly desires and wants.

Sadly, we pray for the things we think we need and become disillusioned when we don't get them.

Help us today to pray to find the abundance and happiness in everything we currently have so that we build space in our lives for more blessings.

Amen.

Day 226

Today's prayer: Lord . . .

Why is it easier to sing the blues? Our attention is often diverted from the blessings we possess by the things we lack.

In other words, what we have is overshadowed by what isn't there. You told us to focus on our gifts and not to worry about our needs, that You'll take care of them.

That is a big step of faith. Take us from baby steps and help us to grow up and walk as adults.

Give us the faith today to realize that those things we lack will be met by the gifts we possess.

Make it easier to sing Your praise than to sing the blues.

Amen.

Day 227

Today's prayer: Lord . . .

There are two things that you long to hear from us and we are often remiss in telling you.

Let us not forget any longer and daily remember to tell you:

Thank you for everything!

and

We love you!

Of all of the blessings that we have received, You and Your love are the greatest.

Amen

Day 228

Today's prayer: Lord . . .

Today is a very special day. For some people it is their birthday, for others their anniversaries.

There will be parties and celebrations in honor of some event of the past. That kind of special is for some of us, but for all of us today is a day You made and gave to us.

Help us to recognize how special that makes today and every day. Today is a special gift that we will someday return. In recognition of this, lift us to celebration so that we are glad and rejoice. Thank You for the gift of today.

Help us to use it to its fullest extent, and help us to remember that this is a day You have made. Let us not only be glad but rejoice.

Amen.

Day 229

Today's prayer: Lord . . .

Thank You for miracles. My hectic life has blinded me to the fact that miracles are all around me, and my consistent inability to see them has made me cynical and faithless.

Restore and grow my faith by opening my eyes to the greatest miracle that has ever occurred—the miracle that carries with it amazing potential, the miracle filled with amazing love, the miracle with the ability to change lives.

Show me the purpose of this miracle and focus it so that it shines brightly in the darkness and people cannot deny Your presence because of it.

Show the world that the greatest miracle is reading this prayer, which we believe is a work of Your hand.

Amen.

Day 230

Today's prayer: Lord . . .

As we reflect on the special occasions when gifts are exchanged, we recall the times when we received a gift that was totally unexpected or undeserved. Many times we cried in joy; then, as we thought deeper, we realized we seldom felt that way when we received the things we asked for.

Lord, our prayers are filled with our asking for blessings and Your help, and we don't only do it to You; we do it to people around us too.

These prayers to You and demands of those around us take away from the special meaning of blessings and gifts. Please forgive us for this selfishness. In our asking of You and others to meet our needs, we lose the greatest gifts given to us.

In our demands we miss the love that is freely shared because they, and You, cared. For love is measured in what is given and not what is received.

Surprise us today with Your blessings. Rather than asking, we wait in faith and trust for the greatest of blessings.

Amen.

Day 231

Today's prayer: Lord ...

We pray in the moment.

At this moment, someone is hurting.

The pain may be physical or mental or emotional.

Touch them kindly and embrace them in Your love.

Comfort them and let feel Your divine presence.

Make them whole again and if need be, let it be through us!

Amen.

Day 232

Today's prayer: Lord . . .

People wrongly believe that if they have more or do more they will be happier. The truth is, they need to be truly happy and grateful before they can do more and receive the desires of their hearts.

Help me not to be like those people.

Change me by showing me how to be truly grateful for the wonderful gifts and blessings I have. Help me to not be distracted by what I think I need or deserve, for those two things are deceptions that only keep me from fully experiencing the joy I could have in this very moment.

Amen.

Day 233

Today's prayer...Lord...

With you we can have lives unlimited and full of miracles...

Our nature is such that we seek explanations and allow our limited minds limit what can and can't be...

Miracles are those things that defy explanation...

Help us to live lives that are ever growing in miracles by helping us to learn to not waste time chasing reasons and explanations...and just enjoying what you have given us...

Thank you for miracles...

Thank you for a child-like faith that does not require explanations...

Amen

Day 234

Today's prayer: Lord . . .

There are times when we feel lost and don't know which way to go. There are times when decisions become difficult and we don't know what to do.

You told us that You are the way, and You told us that all we have to do is follow You.

Help us to remember that there is no easier way. There are no missteps when they come from You.

Amen.

Day 235

Today's prayer: Lord . . .

Thank You for reminding me that "the best things come in threes." I realize that this is just a saying, yet there are three keys that we constantly need to use to effectively live in Your shadow: the master key of prayer, the second key of listening, and the third key of action. We can pray and listen constantly but there is no value unless these are topped off with action.

Show us when and how to move.

Make our actions meaningful and significant. Prayer requires faith, and listening requires trust. These are dead without action.

Help us to learn to trust You and obey Your answers and direction so that in the end we hear, "Good job, faithful servant."

Amen.

Day 236

Today's prayer: Lord . . .

Every one of us goes through times in our lives when we feel emptiness and hunger. You told us to drink of "living water" and eat of the "bread of life."

What are these things? Your answer to this is simple: The water is prayer and the bread is love.

Fill our lives with prayer and love today, and we will never hunger or thirst again!

Amen.

Day 237

Today's prayer: Lord . . .

It's all about keys. We unlock the door to our house and enter. We use a key to start our cars to go where we want to go. We have many different keys for many things.

You are the master and have given us one key to unlock all things.

Our master key is prayer. Help us to use this key to start our day and go where we need to go. Remind us to use it to unlock the door to Your presence. Most of all, show us how to use it to unlock the hearts of others who are bound with shackles to this world.

Prayer is the key. It's in our hands, and it's time we turn it.

Amen.

Day 238

Today's prayer: Lord . . .

Keys serve no purpose unless they are used to open things. Help us to use the keys and our talents that You have given us to unlock those things that separate us and others from You.

Guide the words of our prayers.

Quiet our hearts so that we hear only Your voice.

Spur us to action in Your love.

Help us to change our worlds—at least, the parts that matter.

Amen.

Day 239

Today's prayer: Lord . . .

You came and gave the world hope and it changed.

Thank You.

You gave us the gift of hope and we changed.

Thank You.

Make us beacons of hope to others and to the world today.

Let us be changed with Your hope so that, through our lives, others receive the hope they need to do the same. It is the hope that we possess in the present that seeds the garden of tomorrow.

Plant those seeds within us today and make the harvest bountiful.

Amen.

Day 240

Today's prayer: Lord ...

There are days when we simply have to stop and say thank You.

Today is one of those days.

Let our gratitude go beyond simple words and make it permeate every part of our being so that it affects not only our thoughts and words but our every action.

Help us to truly act just as we would if we were "a prisoner freed"... because we are!

Amen.

Day 241

Today's prayer: Lord . . .

The sun rises and sets every day. The world was created and prospered in its consistency.

Although we can trust the sun to rise and set every day, each sunrise and sunset has its own beauty.

Help us to grasp this lesson, to seek consistency in the right things, at the foundational level of our being. Help us to see the unique beauty of each day, just like the beauty of each sunrise.

Amen.

Day 242

Today's prayer: Lord ...

When things become routine and comfortable, it is easy for us to take it for granted and forget how special it is.

Let us not forget how wonderful You have been in every aspect and detail of our lives.

Help us to keep the awe and wonder of Your grace and love in the forefront of our thoughts, words, and deeds—to the point where we can't help but do what is good, true, and beautiful.

Pour out Your spirit of excitement and energy upon us so that it flows out and touches the lives of others in ways unimaginable.

Amen.

Day 243

Today's prayer: Lord . . .

Thank You for the gifts and talents that You have given us. They were given to us not for our benefit only but also for the benefit of others.

Give us many opportunities today to put our gifts to good use. It is through their use that Your glory and grace are shown and our mission and purpose are found and fulfilled.

Thank You.

Amen.

Day 244

Today's prayer: Lord . . .

We have heard and read about how upset You were with people who talked the talk but walked a different walk. You stressed the importance of "saying and doing and being."

Work with us from today forward. Make our thoughts, words, and actions consistent so that we stop living lies. Let our promises hold. Let our "yes be yes" and our "no be no."

You live through us in our truths, just as the enemy does in lies and intentional failures.

Amen.

Day 245

Today's prayer: Lord . . .

Make us ever more aware of Your presence and our purpose.

Focus our time here on things that will make this world and those around us better for Your having touched their existence through us.

Bless those who have pain and sickness.

Bless those in need.

Bless those who are starting anew.

Bless those who are where they need to be.

You made us to be blessings to all those and more. As unbelievable as that seems, make us a blessing.

Amen.

Day 246

Today's prayer: Lord ...

You taught many valuable lessons using the world around us. You pointed out that the plants, birds, and animals do not worry about tomorrow and are well taken care of because they are doing what they are here to do. They don't know if they will have a tomorrow.

In truth, we don't either. Help us to live today to its fullest, to do what we were put here to do.

Although we all differ in style, we all were designed to love. Let us be the beacon of Your love to those in need of it!

Amen.

Day 247

Today's prayer: Lord . . .

Today we thank You for the people You have brought into our lives—those who are good and those who are bad.

We have learned something from each, and they have made us who we are.

Be with them today, and make it possible for those who need us to open the door to us so that we too can be a blessing to them, as You are to us.

Amen.

Day 248

Today's prayer: Lord . . .

Do not let us forget how special it is to be called Your child. Let that thought humble us and excite us. Make that thought open our eyes to those around us; they are also Your children.

Make that thought remove our anger and judgment. Let it spark in us the desire to leave every moment better for our having been part of it.

Renew in us a desire to make our little worlds better, not for our glory or benefit but for Yours and for those we touch today and tomorrow.

Amen.

Day 249

Today's prayer: Lord . . .

There are so many things that we could be praying for. At times it is overwhelming. We often waste time trying to figure out what to pray about. We do the same thing in our lives. We waste precious time wondering which path we should take.

What matters is that we are praying and walking. You'll make both right.

Today we pray for something or someone, each in our own way. Help us to remember that it is more important to be praying and walking than looking and waiting.

It is through action, any action with good intent, that You can enter the world.

Let Your entry be through us.

Amen.

Day 250

Today's prayer: Lord . . .

Many spend a great portion wandering through life looking for something. They feel lost.

What we need to realize is that to find what we are looking for, we must get lost. We are lost to many of the things of this world, and often to ourselves and what we think we need.

Help us to see clearly those things that are clouding our search.

Remove the barriers and hurdles.

Take away our worries and fears.

Help us to find what we need by getting lost to what we don't need.

Amen.

Day 251

Today's prayer: Lord . . .

Be with those who are sick.

Be with those who are hurting.

Be with the brokenhearted.

Be with those who need Your help.

WAIT.

That's not Your job.

That's our job.

Instead, dear Lord, show us where to go!

Amen.

Day 252

Today's prayer: Lord . . .

Please be with those who suffer from violence and trauma.

Comfort those who are hurting and struggling.

Calm those who are living in senseless drama.

Guide them in ways that only You can.

Make them safe and let them feel the shelter of Your love.

Amen.

Day 253

Today's prayer: Lord . . .

We just want to thank You for the gift of life.

We have no requests.

We have no complaints.

We are just thankful for being alive.

Amen.

Day 254

Today's prayer: Lord . . .

Help us to see that prayer is the most important conversation of the day.

It is important to take EVERYTHING to You before we take it to anyone else.

You are the best listener.

There is no need to cry or scream or yell.

You hear even the most silent prayers.

Most importantly, after our prayers, help us to remember to listen.

Amen.

Day 255

Today's prayer: Lord . . .

Help us to remember that we are designed to learn and grow and share. This is our purpose and mission. Help us to see that everything in life is a lesson.

When we are successful, it is an opportunity to learn to be ever more grateful and humble.

When we fail, we learn to be ever more grateful and persistent.

When we learn, we grow in ways unimaginable.

When we stop learning, we fail to fulfill our purpose.

We are not praying for more opportunities to learn. Instead we pray to learn from the opportunities afforded us. Make us ever more aware of the lessons You intend to teach us.

Amen.

Day 256

Today's prayer: Lord . . .

Everyone has burdens.

Your burden was a cross.

That cross was also a key that opened the doors of heaven to us.

Help us to see that the burdens that we have are also keys that can open the doors of heavens for others.

Unlike You, we do not have to carry our burdens alone.

Walk with us and lighten our load so that we can turn those burdens into blessings, not for us, but for others who struggle.

Amen.

Day 257

Today's prayer: Lord . . .

You made the world around us, and You gave us a simple tool that we can use to change it and the lives of the people in it. As powerful as it is, we often forget to use it or wrongly use it for own selfish desires and ends.

It is prayer.

Thank You for this gift. Help us to first use it, then to use it right, then to strive to be it, just as You were.

Make us not only a prayer but also the answer to a prayer.

Amen.

Day 258

Today's prayer: Lord ...

Thank You for prayer. It is an ointment that soothes our hearts and stands as the foundation for all of the good that happens in our journey. Many great and wonderful things have started with a simple prayer.

Place those prayers in our hearts, and let us be at the beginning of some great and wonderful things.

Amen.

Day 259

Today's prayer: Lord . . .

Your presence changed the world, and it continues to do so today. We are here to do the same.

It is the measure of Your presence in our lives that determines how much our world changes and how much we change the world around us.

The party cannot begin until the host opens the door and invites the guest in.

Today we ask You in with more than words—with our actions, with a smile that brightens someone's day by picking up a piece of trash that we would have stepped over, with a word of encouragement or a compliment, with efforts that leave it better for our having been there.

With a thank You!

Amen.

Day 260

Today's prayer: Lord . . . .

Your will for us is perfect and ours is not. Our will often fights Your will for us.

Today we seek Your will.

We also see that we are often distracted by the allures of this world or the selfish desires of our hearts. Help us to recognize what is right. Help us to do Your will and to stop doing our own will in Your name.

Guide our thoughts, words, and deeds to Your end, not ours.

Amen.

Day 261

Today's prayer: Lord . . .

You command the storms. The winds and the rain stop with Your word. Nature is filled with storms of many types, all in Your control.

Our nature is filled with storms of many types—all in Your control if we let You.

Let Your word resound in our lives so that we walk boldly in peace, to the benefit of all that we touch.

Amen.

Day 262

Today's prayer: Lord . . .

We talk and talk and talk, yet we fail to realize that You have all the answers before we utter our first words.

Today we exercise the seldom used side of prayer.

Today we will LISTEN.

When You talk we will listen—with our hearts, our minds, our eyes, and our ears. We will listen for what You have longed to tell us and we need to hear.

Amen.

Day 263

Today's prayer: Lord . . .

You came so that we could experience abundance, not excess. We have taken that for granted.

Help us to realize that what we have is more than what we need.

Help us to use what is before us to its fullest.

Help us to fully appreciate this gift and act in real gratitude.

Abundance is found in the present, not in the dreams and aspirations of tomorrow.

Dear Lord, be present in our present.

Amen.

Day 264

Today's prayer: Lord . . .

Everything happens for a reason, and that is often all we need to know.

Help us not to waste our time looking for the explanations and just act accordingly in faith and trust—of You and of Your plan for us.

Big things have been accomplished by "little people of faith."

May it be that we change the world, or at least the part that matters. Take the life we think we want and make it into the life we need.

Amen.

Day 265

Today's prayer: Lord . . .

Every moment is a gift. Thank You. An often missed part of life is that those gifts have many layers.

When we are sick we get rest and appreciate our health more completely.

When we are poor we are grateful for what we have. In moments of loneliness we appreciate our friends.

The list is endless.

Help us today to look deeper and closer at our moments and find the hidden blessings in each—each to Your glory.

Amen.

Day 266

Today's prayer: Lord . . .

You are called many things: King of Kings, Prince of Peace, Love, and many more.

Although many do not realize it, You are also known as hope.

In fact, You *are* hope!

Hope is powerful.

Hope is our next breath.

Hope is our next heartbeat.

Hope is fulfillment of our dreams.

Hope is the reason we live.

We need hope to move to tomorrow. We can only achieve our hopes by acting in the present and blindly moving forward to the future.

Help us to plant the good seeds of action today and live to see the harvest of our actions in the future.

Let us harvest hope.

Amen.

Day 267

Today's prayer: Lord . . . .

You are what is good, true, and beautiful in this world. Help us to always see and be part of that.

Although pain, suffering, hunger, hatred, sadness, poverty, and loneliness will always be here, let them not be part of our world, for those things are not from You.

Comfort and protect us from these conditions so that we may be the comfort and protection to others, doing for others as You have done for us.

Drive our actions from our gratitude to You and purely to Your glory.

Amen.

Day 268

Today's prayer: Lord . . .

We get so caught up in our own problems that we forget a very important thing.

Something that You long to hear from us.

Lord, we love You!

Help us to remember to tell you this at every opportunity.

Lord, we love You!

Amen.

Day 269

Today's prayer: Lord ...

Thank You for healing and health.

Be with those who lack these precious gifts and are sick and in pain.

Give them comfort and peace.

Calm their fears and, if it is Your will, heal them so that Your glory and love are shown to an unbelieving world through these miracles, and in the lives that they live—because of You!

Amen.

Day 270

Today's prayer: Lord . . .

My prayer today is different, focused on one simple thing.

Rather than asking for an answer, let me be the answer to someone's prayer today.

Amen.

Day 271

Today's prayer: Lord . . .

Thank You for this wonderful earth. I have all too often taken it for granted.

Forgive me for my failure to recognize this amazing gift.

Use the seeds created by my gratitude and remorse to blossom into the kind of actions that show that this place is special to me.

For now, this earth is my only home. It truly is a miracle that is to be appreciated.

Amen.

Day 272

Today's prayer: Lord . . .

Thank You!

Help me to remember that gratitude itself is a privilege. Gratitude is a gift that You have given to me.

You have opened my eyes to the world around me and to my very existence.

Thank You for this earth. Please awaken within me the desire to help all creatures small and large.

Help me to find ways to protect our earth. Move me to clean up after myself and others. Remind me that I am here to leave my home better for my having been here. It's my only home. I am truly grateful for it, although I often forget to act that way.

Help me to show that gratitude in how I treat this earth.

Amen.

Day 273

Today's prayer: Lord ...

It is all a gift, the good and the bad.

Thank You.

We arise from nothing and we will return to nothing. Everything in between is borrowed from You: who we are, what we have, even the time we have.

EVERYTHING is borrowed, and everything will be returned.

Thank You.

Help us to realize this and give us the passion to make the most of who we are. Give us the passion to make the most of what we have, and give us the passion to make the most of the time we have been given.

As we think deeper, we realize EVERYTHING we have and are is more than a gift, and EVERYTHING is borrowed and will be returned.

Thank You.

Amen.

Day 274

Today's prayer: Lord . . .

You have made each of us rich in our own way—rich in gratitude, rich in praise, rich in worship—yet all of our actions fall short of what You deserve.

We lack the infinite abilities we need to repay You for what we have been given.

Yet we possess one meager thing that we can offer to You for what You have done for us: our love. Take it and make it grow.

Increase our love of this earth, its plants, its animals, and its people so that this miracle of life continues to Your glory.

Amen.

Day 275

Today's prayer: Lord . . .

Everything in life is small and fleeting, yet at the same time everything in life is one and eternal.

Thank You for moments—moments of sadness that make happy times all the better, moments of pain that make health amazing, moments of hunger and poverty to remind us of our riches, moments of loneliness that show us how precious love is.

Everything in life is good and wonderful when taken in its entirety. Help us not to look upon the moment for anything other than the gift it is.

Every moment is the seasoning to enhance the flavor of what is to come. Each moment is the feast of celebration for a life well lived.

Thank You.

Amen.

Day 276

Today's prayer: Lord . . .

I have everything that I need to make today everything it needs to be.

Failure is no one's fault but my own.

Help me to focus on the right things at the right time, for the right reason.

In doing this, I'll find the fulfillment, peace, and happiness that I seek.

Amen.

Day 277

Today's prayer: Lord . . .

When You walked this earth You did not do so in search of blessings, but rather looking to be a blessing.

In living this way, You trusted Your every need to be fulfilled, and they were.

Help me to do the same.

I pray to seek and be a blessing to the world around me, not for selfish gain but from a heart of love and gratitude for the blessings I already possess and for what I am.

Amen.

Day 278

Today's prayer: Lord . . .

I am meant to grow All things happen for a purpose, good or bad.

Help me to realize that nothing is lasting and that when I am aligned with You, everything leads to a good end. I succeed at some things or I learn something; in either case, I grow as You planned for me to grow.

Thank You for the successes in my life, and thank You for the lessons that I have learned through my failures!

Help each and every moment work to the benefit of the world around me—or at least the part that matters.

Amen.

Day 279

Today's prayer: Lord . . .

There is a time for all things These things or events serve one of two purposes: They are the reward for our work or they are preparation for the future.

From this perspective, we thank You for making our present a present.

Help me to truly appreciate what my present means to me—both what I have been given and have, and what I have not been given and I do not have.

Each has been given or not given to me in love.

Today move me to act for Your benefit and Your glory.

Amen.

Day 280

Today's prayer: Lord . . .

Thank You for answers. Answers to my every question are out there.

Some answers are apparent, some are subtler, and still others are found in the fact that I don't get them.

It is my nature to seek answers whether I need them or not. Help me not to be deceived into believing something that is not because it is the answer I want, but to see each and every situation for what it is.

Make me a person of faith.

Help me to see every situation as it is and to move on, in real faith and hope, so that I am not wasting my precious time and energy on things that are not real.

Amen.

Day 281

Today's prayer: Lord . . .

You gave Your life so that I might live abundantly. Thank You. I live an abundant life through how I give unselfishly.

Help me to realize that the measure of my fulfillment in this world is not in how much I am loved by others but in how much I share the love You loaned to me with others.

May this knowledge spark the right acts so that each day someone's life is better for the love I have shared.

Amen.

Day 282

Today's prayer: Lord . . . .

I pray for my mother, Mother Earth, a precious gift that gives me life while I often treat her ungratefully.

Thank You for giving her to me.

Thank You for her selfless love.

I pray that I may be more like her each and every day, and I pray for those I love.

May I be more like Your glorious creation to them.

Amen.

Day 283

Today's prayer: Lord . . .

"For by God's grace you have been saved by faith."

"If you had faith the size of a mustard seed, you could say to a mountain, 'Get into the ocean,' and it would happen."

Even deeper and more special than my salvation being a free gift, I realize that my faith is a gift too.

Thank You for faith.

I pray for faith, but are the fruits of faith and trust manifest in my life?

Am I trusting? If so, then worry should be nonexistent in my life, for I trust in You!

Am I patient? If so, then I should not be impatient with Your perfect timing. Things will happen when You have planned them.

Today I pray not for faith but for the fruits of faith to be manifest in my life, so that I can truly experience the "joy of salvation," for it is then that miracles happen to Your glory and for the salvation of others.

Amen.

Day 284

Today's prayer: Lord . . .

This world is in dire need of a wakeup call. It has grown complacent and narrow-visioned in its thoughts, words, and actions. It needs its eyes opened and its heart and spirit refreshed.

Am I part of this world, or am I "in it but not of it"?

Let this renewal begin today, and let it begin with me.

Let the spirit of this carry throughout the year so that the joy of life and giving becomes a way of life rather than an isolated event.

Amen.

Day 285

Today's prayer: Lord . . .

Prayer is a wonderful gift. Thank You.

Unlike most other gifts and talents, prayer was given freely to everyone. Prayer is to my soul not unlike what breathing is to my body. This should not point to its insignificance but to its importance. Like a body cannot live without breathing, a soul cannot live without prayer.

Help me to use this gift properly and often. Help me to use prayer to its fullest potential rather than superficially.

Today I pray to be an answer to prayer and a blessing rather than simply praying and asking for blessings, for this is a higher aspiration.

Thank You for this wonderful insight.

Amen.

Day 286

Today's prayer: Lord . . .

What is my purpose?

I bet You hear this question often. As I look to the words that You left with us and consider nature itself, I realize the answer may be hiding in plain sight!

Although Your parable of the sower and the seeds is about Your Word and the different types of people who hear it, we forget the fact that "in the beginning was the Word and the word was with God and the Word was God."

Yes, the seeds are the Word, the seeds are You, and the seeds are us!

We are seeds, or we should be!

As I consider seeds, I see that each seed contains all the experience and adaptations of its ancestors. A seed is covered and protected from the elements of the present and carries with it nutrition for its future!

My purpose is to be a seed. Plant me, dear Lord, in fertile soil so that I may bear fruit that serves You, my friends, and my family, all to Your glory.

Amen.

Day 287

Today's prayer: Lord . . .

You are the potter and we are the clay. From the very beginnings of our lives, You began to mold us into vessels with a specific shape and with a specific purpose.

Give us the opportunity to change this world according to Your plan and Your glory.

Amen.

Day 288

Today's prayer: Lord . . .

Thank You for the blessing of another day and all the wonderful things that it affords.

Help me not to squander a minute of the blessing and to be a miracle to someone today.

Although I seek comfort and love, let me be the comfort and love to another.

Help me to remember that it is in giving that I receive fullness of life.

Let the blessings flow, and let the blessing be me!

Amen.

Day 289

Today's prayer: Lord . . .

I pray that today You pour out the greatest gifts upon this earth in excess—gifts of love and comfort, peace and healing, protection and kindness.

Touch those in greatest need so that they feel these gifts and know that someone is praying for them.

I am here to live, experience, and share my gifts. It is through me that these gifts manifest themselves in the world.

Let them be here and real, in me and through me.

Amen.

Day 290

Today's prayer: Lord . . .

You are the beginning and the end and everything in between, the alpha and omega. Thank You.

Open my eyes and heart to Your presence in all things that are good, true, and beautiful.

Help me to remember that I am a steward and guardian of this world and the people in it. I am here to serve and not be served; I am here to love and not be loved; I am here to comfort and not be comforted.

The abundance You promised is not in what I receive but in what I give.

Even though all things are possible, help me to narrow my vision and chase only the things that serve You and my mission, not those things that reject You or me.

It is in this simplicity that I will find what You have promised.

Amen.

Day 291

Today's prayer: Lord . . .

Thank You for this day. It is a wonderful gift.

Help me to face its challenges and overcome them.

Help me to savor the victories and learn from the failures.

All things work to glory for those who love You.

Most of all, help me to love You more today than I did yesterday.

Amen.

Day 292

Today's prayer: Lord . . .

You made us to be the salt of this world. We, by Your plan, are meant to be its flavor. Thank You for this role in the cosmic drama.

It is strange how we often sit in wonder, asking ourselves what has gone wrong.

Why has this world become so selfish?

Why are people so nasty?

Why are people so hurtful?

Why are people so bitter?

The fact is, we fail to realize that this flavor has been made by us—by what we have done and, more important, by what we have failed to do.

You not only made us "the salt"; You told us that You did. And You told us that this responsibility did not come without a warning.

You also told us that salt that loses its flavor will be spread on the roads and paths and walked upon.

Thank You.

Place these two pieces of knowledge firmly in our hearts today.

Let them ignite the right thoughts and actions so that we are lifted up by what we say and do rather than walked upon by the world we have created.

Amen.

Day 293

Today's prayer: Lord . . .

Every day is a gift and, more important, a chance to be different. Thank You.

Each day I move closer to the happiness You have planned for me and further away from the pains and sorrows of the past. Thank You.

Every moment is potentially life-changing for me. Make the changes happen in me and for me.

Yet I ask that You give me opportunities to also change others' lives today, and the time to enjoy the fullness of the moment of change in them and in me. For it is when I set out to change lives and I allow You to do so through me that my life is changed the most—and all to Your glory because I love You!

Amen.

Day 294

Today's prayer: Lord . . .

Every day is filled to overflowing with blessings, but often, in our haste and nearsightedness, we fail to see them.

Today we realize that the first blessing is that not all blessings are readily apparent. We have to look for them. This makes our lives interesting, challenging, and worth living.

Open our eyes and hearts.

Help us find more and more blessings, and let not a day go by without a new discovery of Your wonderful love for us.

The blessings are there. We just have to find them.

Amen.

Day 295

Today's prayer: Lord . . .

You are the greatest of all teachers. Thank You.

Thank You for teaching me in so many different ways.

Thank You for being patient with me.

Thank You for looking out for my safety.

Bring to mind all of the things that I should be thankful for.

Make me conscious of all that I have received and of all that I haven't.

Help me to see and believe that both are gifts, for it is through gratitude for everything that I truly learn the lessons that will lead me to abundance, and to living an authentically happy life.

Amen.

Day 296

Today's prayer: Lord . . .

I am a creature of habit. I may not realize it, but I am completely defined and known by my habits. Some are good and some are bad.

Not a day goes by when I do not desire to change one or more of those habits that I want to stop doing. Although I desire change, most of the time I fail.

I pray that You help me to turn the tides of failure by opening my eyes to the real secret to change.

Help me to see that habits cannot be stopped; they must be replaced.

Help me to find and repeat new and better things, and to focus on that.

Make these good activities more than a onetime occurrence. Make them good habits that take over and leave no room for bad habits to happen.

Help me to replace the habit of fear with prayer.

Help me to replace poverty by living in acts of abundance.

Help me to leave no room for sadness by increasing happiness the in my life.

Leave no room for sickness by showing me how to engage in more healthy activities.

Remove the hatred and anger by giving me more opportunities to love.

This is the secret that will make this year the best year yet, one lived to Your glory.

Thank You.

Amen.

Day 297

Today's prayer: Lord . . .

In our love for and dedication to You, we seek Your will for our lives. Too often we get so focused on seeking the plan for our lives that we never do what You want us to do.

Help us to simply act with good and pure intent, making every word and deed spring from love.

Let us leave the rest to You. Your glory becomes real through the faithful acts. Let us act in faith. It is what You said: "Tomorrow has its own set of worries."

Let us focus on today.

Amen.

Day 298

Today's prayer: Lord . . .

We often pray for miracles, looking for Your immediate intervention to change inevitable outcomes.

Help us to realize that miracles take on many different forms, to the point where we should see that everything in our lives is a miracle.

We thank You for miracles and pray that You make our entire life a miracle, as it should be, to the benefit of others and to Your glory.

Amen.

Day 299

Today's prayer: Lord . . .

Let me live a life that could be described as an autumn leaf being carried along on a river of faith.

Let us dance like that leaf with peace, joy, and freedom, knowing that there is but one destination.

Let me not lose sight of the fact that every current and eddy is temporary and simply adds to the beauty of the dance.

Thank You, for all of creation points to You and some of the greatest lessons can be seen in nature—but only by those who have the eyes to see the messages.

Open my eyes to more of these messages each day.

Amen.

Day 300

Today's prayer: Lord . . .

There is a reason that the here and now is called our "present." It is a gift from You.

We have no idea what tomorrow will be like, and our concerns and worries over the future only drain the blessings from this moment. As narrow and naive as this may sound, it is what You taught when You walked among us.

Help us to be ever grateful and to radiate beauty like the lilies of the fields and sing merry songs like the sparrows.

For You promised that if we keep our eyes on our present, our Father will take care of us better than we could ever imagine.

Thank You for sharing this wonderful wisdom with us. Give us the faith to act upon it and truly understand and enjoy our present.

Amen.

Day 301

Today's prayer: Lord . . .

I have lived with so many blessings for so long that I take them for granted. Many of them were made possible through sacrifices of truly dedicated and loving individuals.

Let not their deaths be in vain. "No greater love can a person show but by dying for the ones he or she loves."

Most important, let me not forget and help me to fully appreciate the sacrifice You made for us. No greater love can be expressed. You died for me, and You have set me free.

Amen.

Day 302

Today's prayer: Lord . . .

In many of our prayers we ask for blessings. Less often we pray to be a blessing.

The reasons for this are many, yet we are here to be blessings to our world and not to be blessed! This is our purpose.

Today we pray that You work in our lives in such a way as to remove our excuses for not living to that purpose and mission. We can pray unceasingly to be a blessing, but one simple excuse can kill this important prayer.

Let us not stand in the way of Your glorious plans for us.

Amen.

Day 303

Today's prayer: Lord . . .

"Why?" is a powerful question.

When directed to others it opens the doors to judgment.

When directed to You it is the clay questioning the potter's intent, and it opens the doors to rebellion.

When directed inward it opens the doors to growth.

When it is not asked it opens the doors to trust and faith.

Help us to use "Why?" appropriately and not allow it to open doors that need to remain shut.

Amen.

Day 304

Today's prayer: Lord . . .

There are times when we don't feel like praying and doing. That is when we ask that You pray for us and with us. It is also a time when we look for You to work in our lives and keep us moving forward.

Persistence is more than our individual prayers and efforts.

It is to be our makeup and nature.

It is You working through us and our allowing it.

It is inspired. It is Your living through us.

Help us to hold true to the gift of persistence and use it to Your glory.

Amen.

Day 305

Today's prayer: Lord . . .

We search for truth. We search for facts.

We direct our lives and live based on what we believe to be truth and fact, yet we do not realize that You are the only real truth.

We forget that You told us that You are "the way, the truth, and the life." All else in this world and what we hold as true fades in comparison to You.

You are the path to the Father. Help us to look to You as the truth and the way to living the life we were meant to live. Help us to stop seeking truths that only lead to our destruction and that take others away from You!

Amen.

Day 306

Today's prayer: Lord . . .

It is in our nature to want more and to want something different. Although this drives us to higher levels of being, it also causes us to miss the most wonderful blessings that are at our door.

Open our eyes. Help us to see the people whom You have put on our path and all of the wonderful gifts we already possess. Except for You, nothing waits forever. It's all borrowed.

Let us not lose the gifts or the people in our lives because we failed to recognize them, failed to act, or failed to show our appreciation for them.

Lord, the biggest sense of failure and regret comes when we realize how close to success we were when we quit or failed to see the truth and act, and we realize what we lost. That which was on loan and returned will never again grace our lives. Help us to learn from our mistakes.

Count our blessings and keep us from that regret by moving us to action.

Amen.

Day 307

Today's prayer: Lord . . .

It only takes a spark to start a warming fire. That's how it is with love. We can be paying it back or we can be paying it forward.

In truth, it doesn't matter what the reason is for what we do. What matters is that we look for and do something to make someone's life a little better because we love.

Open our eyes to the people who need help. We will do it because we love You and we love them.

Amen.

Day 308

Today's prayer: Lord . . .

You are who You are.

We are who we are.

You saw us completely as part of Your plan before creation because of who You are.

We were not created simply by chance because of who You are.

We see You dimly because of who we are.

We are part of Your perfect plan because of who You are.

You made us to love You freely because of who You are.

Help us to fulfill Your plan for us. Keep us safe. Help us make a difference because of who You are.

Amen.

Day 309

Today's prayer: Lord . . .

The world, our world, is what it is. What we see is our perceptions and a matter of our interpretation. Our interpretation is guided by our attitude.

Help us to constantly be of positive attitude so that we see the beauty of this world and not miss the majesty and gifts that are around us.

When this change takes place in our lives, we are truly blessed.

Amen.

Day 310

Today's prayer: Lord . . .

Since we were children we dreamed of living happily ever after. Our minds set our vision and goals on the future.

It's good to dream. It's good to set goals. It's good to want and hunger.

My father used to tell me, "As much as tomorrow could be better, it could be worse."

Help us to be grateful for today and what we have.

Our lives become much more complete when we focus on the gifts we have been given rather than building our "happily ever afters" upon fleeting wishes and our own impossible dreams.

Yet let us remember and hold fast to the promise that all things are possible with You. The key to possibility is not what we do or want but You and Your perfect will.

Help us to find the key to possibility.

Amen.

Day 311

Today's prayer: Lord . . .

There are only two reasons that we do what we do: to serve ourselves and our desires, needs, and hungers and to serve You. It is obvious which reason we should have for every action.

Drive our lives from the seeds of our behavior.

Make Your desires our desires. Make Your needs our needs. Make Your hungers our hungers.

Draw us closer to You through this change so that each day Your purpose, our mission, is more completely served.

Amen.

Day 312

Today's prayer: Lord . . .

It's important to pray, but it's also important to listen. And it's most important to do something about it.

Balance each of our days so that we are doing what we are supposed to be doing—praying when it is important, watching and listening when we are to do that, and acting on Your direction when the time is exactly right.

The abundant life is found in the proper combination of all these things and not in the achievement of a single aspect.

Broaden our senses and understanding so that we hunger, then ask, then look and listen. Then move us through trust in Your promise to us so that we will live life and do so abundantly.

Amen.

Day 313

Today's prayer: Lord . . .

There are times when I realize that there are things You look for from me that I look for from others around me!

You delight in Your children, like when a mother is touched when her child hands her a flower or when a father hears, "Look what I can do, Daddy!"

I want to be a source of Your delight. Help me to realize that it requires not a major accomplishment but simple acts, for just one simple reason. . . .

The reason?

I did it because I love You, God. Look at me. Look what I did for You, not because it gets me anything special but just because I love You!

Amen.

Day 314

Today's prayer: Lord . . .

You are my Father. I am also the offspring of my earthly parents and carry their genetics. I am often told that I look like my father and mother. I may have their eyes or body type, yet I am Your child too.

Make my words and deeds such that when people look at me, they see You.

I want Your eyes to see others as You see them.

I want Your heart to drive my actions and decisions in love.

I want Your voice, which comforts, commands, heals, and protects.

I want to share Your love.

I want to be Your hands and feet so that when others see me, they know that I was sent by You.

And they know You by what I do.

And they see You in what I do.

Amen.

Day 315

Today's prayer: Lord . . .

With You I can live my life unlimited. My nature is such that I seek explanations for everything and allow my limited mind to limit what can and can't be.

Miracles are those things that defy explanation.

Help me to live my life such that it is ever growing in miracles by helping me to learn to not waste time chasing reasons and explanations.

Help me to simply enjoy what You have given me.

My life is a miracle. I am a miracle!

Thank You for miracles.

Thank You for me!

Amen.

Day 316

Today's prayer: Lord . . .

Through You there is renewal. Just as the rain cleanses the earth, Your presence in my life cleans and restores me.

Help me to welcome the rain as a gift.

Help me to look skyward and feel the soothing touch of each drop.

Help me to look on Your presence as both the rain and the sun.

Your love is amazing and is a warming, cleansing, and restoring gift. Never let me take them for granted.

Amen.

Day 317

Today's prayer: Lord . . .

Nothing happens by chance. EVERYTHING that happens is by Your perfect design.

Please do not let our limited perspectives and weaknesses stand in the way of our experiencing the fullness of life.

Do not let the baggage that I call my past, and that I refuse to cast off, weigh me down and slow my progress.

The fullness of life is found by looking with new eyes and hearing with new ears.

Make me into a new—and most important, better—creature.

Amen.

Day 318

Today's prayer: Lord . . .

What should I fear?

The answer is simple: nothing!

That answer becomes real when I put the past and the future in the proper perspective. The past is gone and the price had been paid.

The future is nothing but conjecture. Help me to focus on the greatest gift of life: the present of the present!

In doing so, I give the past value based on what I have learned, and the future is controlled by the wisdom of today.

Help me to make the right choices today so that my future, the one You long for me to have, starts tomorrow.

Amen.

Day 319

Today's prayer: Lord . . .

It is through You that my prayers are heard. My prayers become real when they align with Your will. Your will enters my life when the Holy Spirit inspires me.

Control my thoughts and guide my heart.

Inspire me so that every prayer perfectly matches Your plan.

Make my prayers Your prayers.

Make my actions Your actions, so that I leave every moment better for my being there, through You and Your plan.

Amen.

Day 320

Today's prayer: Lord ...

You knew me before creation. This means I am here with Your intent.

Yet I often struggle with anger, hurt, regret, and my past. Create in me a clean heart that loves You and give me a spirit that hears Your voice and follows You.

I love You because You loved us first.

Amen.

Day 321

Today's prayer: Lord . . .

Your love is like the ocean—broad, deep, and mostly unexplored.

I cannot move to higher levels without stepping into the water.

Make me a vessel of love.

Fill me to overflowing so that Your love spills out, touching the lives of others while satisfying my needs and healing my every ill.

Amen.

Day 322

Today's prayer: Lord . . .

It is through You that I can experience the change and growth I desire.

Help me to find ways to open my eyes and heart so that I become a different creature, rising closer and closer to You and experiencing the real fulfillment, success and, impact that only a few have had in the past—all for Your glory.

Amen.

Day 323

Today's prayer: Lord . . .

You are life and life abundant. I am the result of Your patient, quiet, and unseen intervention.

Thank You for everything You have done in all of my yesterdays, because it is all of my yesterdays that have made my today possible.

Help me to live less distracted. Remove all things trivial and allow me to rise to new and higher levels through new and higher experiences.

I know that the gifts are there.

I simply have to open my eyes and take them.

Amen.

Day 324

Today's prayer: Lord . . .

You are compassion. The world needs more compassion, and the sad thing is that we are both the problem and the answer.

You have placed opportunities to rise to higher levels of compassion in our path, yet we hesitate and miss our chances to grow. This important aspect will be made manifest when we cast off the frivolous and we simply act in more loving ways.

Help us to see and embrace both of the opportunities.

Give us opportunities for compassion and opportunities to stop doing the things that take us from our compassionate call. Make us boldly act so that we rise to a higher level of Your love and, as a result, the world becomes more like what it needs to be.

Amen.

Day 325

Today's prayer: Lord . . .

All of life is a race. Whether we realize it or not, we run alone. Yet we cannot win without the help of others and Your help.

My course has many twists and turns.

Guide me in my run so that my path becomes straight and smooth.

Bring the right people into my life who can take me to higher levels of victory, experience, and effectiveness.

Although the finish line is far off, help me to see it clearly and not take my eyes off of it so that I am driven to run my race to win.

Amen.

Day 326

Today's prayer: Lord . . .

With You, every moment has intent and meaning. Help me to find it so that I am not like those who profess to know yet are nothing but fools.

I am not a fool because I follow You. I am not weak because I follow You. I do not fail because I follow You.

I follow You in trust and love, and I am proud to be called Your child.

Today I put Your name on everything I do. Every tick of the clock is meant to have divine purpose. Every beat of my heart is by Your plan. Let not one moment be a waste.

Help me to find that meaning and act upon it!

Amen.

Day 327

Today's prayer: Lord . . .

Your greatest gift to me is forgiveness. This is the single gift in which Your wish for me is that I do not use it for myself; You intend for me to use it on others without hesitation, just as You have forgiven me.

More important, help me not to use forgiveness as a fool would. Separate me from those who would take advantage of this wonderful gift.

Constantly remind me of the power and beauty of this gift.

Thank You for this gift. It is upon this gift that my entire life and my abundance are built.

Amen.

Day 328

Today's prayer: Lord . . .

You are infinite; I, on the other hand, am limited.

I look to grow and serve, but I seldom realize just how limited I am.

Help me to realize that for me to experience something new, something more, or a change, I must remove something from my life.

Letting go is just as important to my growth as is the change that I seek.

Help me to rightly order my life so that I am a perfect combination, doing the right things in the right amounts, at the right time and for the right reasons, from this day forward.

Amen.

Day 329

Today's prayer: Lord . . .

Past, present, and future are all one in Your eyes.

What I was, what I am, and what I will be are the same.

Why? Because of Your love and forgiveness.

Although I wake to a new day and see myself as a new creature, the truth is, it is already a second chance—a chance to show my love for You by sharing it with others.

Help me not to squander the opportunities You have given me.

Make my second chance count before my second chances run out!

Amen.

Day 330

Today's prayer: Lord . . .

There are two things that You long to hear from me and that I am often remiss in telling You.

Let me not forget any longer. Help me remember to thank You for everything and tell You that I love You.

Of all of the blessings I have received, You and Your love are the greatest.

Amen.

Day 331

Today's prayer: Lord . . .

Your word tells us to "be thankful in all things." It is difficult for me to do this, yet it is the key.

I need to be thankful for the victories in my life, for they confirm that I am on the right path.

I need to be thankful for the challenges and failures, for they teach me valuable lessons and lead me to victory later in my life.

I need to be more thankful for the things I have received, for they have made my life possible.

I need to be thankful for the things I have not received, for they show how much You really love me.

Whatever the case, I am thankful to realize that I am on the right path.

Thank You for all things.

Amen.

Day 332

Today's prayer: Lord . . .

How can I become more thankful? Simply by becoming more aware of the blessings around me!

Many times it is the nature of blessings to be hidden and obscure, and it's my challenge to find them so that I can reap the energy that each blessing supplies.

Open my eyes to today's blessings.

Renew my spirit and help me move forward to Your glory and that of others, for of all the blessings that surround me, You are the greatest blessing to me.

Amen.

Day 333

Today's prayer: Lord ...

I want things to change. I have desired change in many aspects of my life. Yet throughout my life I have resisted the very things I longed for because I feared what I would lose if I changed.

I desire change. Let the first change in my life be the elimination of that selfish fear—the fear of loss. Give me the vision, strength, and courage to open my eyes to the reality of what I would gain from the changes in my life.

Help me never to grow complacent or comfortable with how I am. Change is a fact of life.

Let the changes be the right ones, so that I grow as You planned and my every action is to Your glory.

I will continue to change until the day I join You in heaven.

Amen.

Day 334

Today's prayer: Lord . . .

I do not see everything that goes on, nor can I even hope to. I do not know everything that I need to know, nor can I even hope to.

These two situations would be important only if I were alone. Thank You, for I am not alone.

You have these important things under control. All I need is faith, trust, prayer, and an open heart, all of which I have been given.

Help me not to get bound by the need to know or the need to see. Help me to walk in faith, trusting You, asking for guidance, listening for the answer, and acting with love.

I will never take these precious gifts for granted. I will use them as intended, with love for You and for those around me.

Amen.

Day 335

Today's prayer: Lord . . .

You are the reason for everything. I often strive to be more like You. Although that is a commendable goal, it is not what You want.

You want me to be me, plain and simple. Help me to realize that I have purpose, not to be You but to be me. And if there is one thing I learn from You, it is love, for You are love.

Help me to remember that it's not "What would Jesus do?"

It is "What would God have me do?"

Amen.

Day 336

Today's prayer: Lord . . .

Your truths are plain and simple, and I was built to take in those truths with what I see, hear, touch, taste, and feel.

I was built to find You and learn, and not to simply take in that information and keep it to myself.

You want me to allow the truths to affect my mind and heart and to show these changes in my actions—to spread the knowledge to others who, in turn, do the same.

Answers are only given to those who seek. Answers are only given to those who ask questions.

Help me never to become complacent in my quest. Spur questions and give me clarity of senses so that knowledge comes quickly. I ask this so that I can be part of the great learning experience and bring others into it also!

Amen.

Day 337

Today's prayer: Lord . . .

There are times when I am a learner.

There are times when I am a teacher.

I have been given knowledge through my experiences, not just for my own benefit but also to help others. Every day is a learning experience and also an opportunity to teach.

Help me to make the most of each moment by learning what I can and using what I have learned to help others.

It is through the learning and teaching cycle of giving that I will fulfill my purpose and Your plan!

Amen.

Day 338

Today's prayer: Lord . . .

The biggest blessings are often found in the smallest things. I am often blind to those details. You told us that we simply have to seek the kingdom and the rest will be added.

That small blessing is the greatest one.

Thank You, thank You, thank You!

Today my heart and mind will be focused on the kingdom. I need nothing more, for all else pales in comparison to that great gift.

With this blessing I will fly on the eagle's wings and carry Your message to everyone I meet today!

Amen.

Day 339

Today's prayer: Lord . . .

I look to You as the model of how I should be.

You are patient. My faith and trust in You are manifested in this world as patience.

In my heart I know what I need to be. I know how to ask. Yet it seems like I want everything now.

Today I commit to acting with both a sense of intensity and with patience rather than a sense of urgency. With this simple change I will better model my faith, and my actions will lead me to the abundance and happiness You promised.

Amen.

Day 340

Today's prayer: Lord . . .

You came to this world for a single purpose. I too have a single purpose, although my purpose is not the same as Yours was.

Our response to our call should not be any different. You saw Your purpose clearly and stayed true to it. I desire to see mine as clearly as You did!

Most of the time I do not see clearly. I often seem to walk aimlessly.

Today I pray that when I am in the "fog," these are the times I will walk in faith. I know that there is a path of clear vision; I simply need to look up to You and listen to Your direction.

You have given to me all I need to be successful. I commit all that I am to my walk.

I will learn that it is often my unrealistic expectations that are clouding my path.

Amen.

Day 341

Today's prayer: Lord . . .

You are the giver of life. Whether I fully realize it or not, everything I have and am is from You.

Yet I look at myself and want something more or something different. Sadly, I am often an ungrateful child.

I want this to change.

From today forward I commit to using the gifts I have been given to do great and wonderful things rather than looking to do different things with a different life.

One day I must give my life, and everything that it is, back to You. Everything including my life is borrowed, and You will look at what I have done with it and say, "Good job. You have left the world—or at least the part that matters—better for having used it."

May what I have be returned to You be well used according to Your purpose!

Amen.

Day 342

Today's prayer: Lord . . .

There are days that go just as we planned and you stand patiently aside and allow us to enjoy the fruits of harvest.

There are other days that we need you more than ever before and you stand up for us!

On days like that, bring peace to our confusion.

On days like that, bring joy into our sadness.

On days like that, bring hope into our hearts.

The fact of the matter is whether it goes as planned or the day goes poorly, we need you more than ever before.

Stand up for us.

Amen.

Day 343

Today's prayer: Lord . . .

References to nature have often been used in Your lessons. Many wrongly believe that the reason You used stories about nature was that it was something we could really relate to and understand.

The fact is that nature knows the truth and follows the immutable laws without exception.

Oh, if we could only be like this. If we act as nature does, all of the lessons You wish for us to learn are there. All we have to do its look and listen.

With Your help and loving patience, we commit to looking and listening to the messages around us each day.

We will not to be satisfied until we learn something that brings us closer to You and makes our walk easier.

Amen.

Day 344

Today's prayer: Lord . . .

The life that I have is a gift, my greatest gift, one that I often do not recognize.

Today I stop and thank You for my life, and in gratitude commit to being diligent in not squandering this blessing.

Help me to see what I can do to make the most of it and then to do it.

I ask this so that when I have to return it to You, its value will have grown by ten thousand times and You can say, That was a good one. Well spent."

Amen.

Day 345

Today's prayer: Lord ...

Forgiveness is a gift. Forgiveness is something I should never take for granted.

The first time we make a mistake or fail, there is a myriad of good excuses.

Forgiveness gave me a deserved second chance when I came with a contrite heart. But the second time I see that my failure is a choice and no longer falls within the realm of forgiveness.

When I see my transgression of You or others for what it is, I should see that I have simply become a user of Your or another person's love or caring. I look to that person for something he or she should not have to put up with.

This problem can be a deep spiritual sickness that only You can heal. Please begin the healing process as I commit from this day forward to work diligently with a new awareness of how my failures hurt You and others.

Amen.

Day 346

Today's prayer: Lord . . .

Your knowledge is unlimited; mine is not.

Your plan is perfect; mine is not.

You know what I should be doing; I do not.

Today I commit all of my actions to Your plan.

Please give me the knowledge to do and say the things that make You happy with me. Help me to do those things You'd have me do better and not do those things that do not serve my purpose and plan.

I wish to make You proud and show that I truly love You.

Amen.

Day 347

Today's prayer: Lord . . .

I only have to look to nature to get a glimpse of Your majesty.

Nature shouts praises to You and can be heard by those who truly listen. I will take time to stop, look, and listen.

Reveal to me the wonders.

Allow me to join in with nature in its praise of You so that the very foundation of my being knows that You are God.

Amen.

Day 348

Today's prayer: Lord . . .

Past, present, and future are all one in Your eyes. I am often told that the way to live is to release the past, live in the present moment, and not worry about the future. This sounds like great direction, but it is not how You see things.

Help me to bring all three together in my life so that I look on all of my past with gratitude, my present with intense focus, and my future with caring wisdom. In doing so, I make these three important characteristics of love manifest in my actions, changing lives and the parts of the world that matter.

This is when I will see the world as You see it—and, more important to me, with You in it.

Amen.

Day 349

Today's prayer: Lord . . .

With You for me, nothing can be against me.

The measure of my fulfillment and happiness is in direct proportion to how much I submit to Your will and allow You to intervene in every aspect of my existence.

Today I commit Your name and presence to everything I do and say. Make today my best day ever and tomorrow even better.

Amen.

Day 350

Today's prayer: Lord . . .

Your abundance is poured out to me without measure, and You know exactly what I can endure and what I cannot.

My best interests and Your perfect plan are always served. Your love is always in abundance, yet I do not always feel that abundance.

Why not?

It is because I look at the gifts and judge them ungratefully. I say, "Is that all?" or I refuse to accept the gifts, fully or at all.

From today forward I commit to looking to You with gratitude. It is through gratitude to You that the abundant life is made manifest in me and in the world.

Amen.

Day 351

Today's prayer: Lord . . .

Today I will consider the lilies and the sparrows, as You told me to do. I see that their worlds are designed to meet their every need.

The lilies and sparrows lack for nothing and flourish. They sing the songs they were designed to sing and silently share beauty without a word! They are wonderful creations, yet I do not see lilies in a desert or sparrows in the ocean.

I am not unlike the lilies or the sparrows. I lack for nothing when I abide in the world You intended for me to live in. It is when I try to leave that world that I wither or starve.

Help me to commit to learning this important lesson. I must not desire to be different but seek to be the best of Your intent for me.

Lilies do not seek to be roses. Sparrows do not desire to be eagles. Each seeks to be the best lilies and sparrows. They grow and flourish in the world they are in.

When I act on this lesson, it becomes the start of my showing the world that I love You and believe in Your lordship over my life.

You made this world and made it possible for me in it.

Thank You, thank You, THANK YOU!

Amen.

Day 352

Today's prayer: Lord . . .

Everything is beyond my comprehension, yet I continue to ask, "Why?"

Regardless of the situation, the answer is the same.

Today I commit to acting on that single answer.

What answer?

The answer is: "Because You love me!"

Thank You for that answer and for Your love. Even that is beyond my understanding. Please accept my meager love in return.

Amen.

Day 353

Today's prayer: Lord . . .

There are times for everything—times to work, times to rest, and times to stop and tell You, "Thank You."

Guide my decisions so that I am doing the right things at the right time, for even the best work is useless when not done at the right time.

At this moment I stop and say thank You, not just from my mind but from my heart.

At this moment I stop to rest and recognize Your love for me.

With this simple activity set, I will be refilled, renewed, reenergized, and guided to do the right things.

Amen.

Day 354

Today's prayer: Lord . . .

In all things I wish to seek what is important first and not worry about anything else. Yet I am often confused and overwhelmed by the world around me. The only connection I have with the world around me is my senses and my interpretation of them.

And what I see and hear is always a matter of my interpretation. Right or wrong, it is for me and me alone. Your world is beyond my senses and a matter of my heart first. I will never see or hear it while I am here. There is no interpretation; it is beyond my senses and intellect.

Make Your world real in my heart so that what I seek is what I see clearly, so that all else is just an added benefit.

Amen.

Day 355

Today's prayer: Lord . . .

Enough is enough. You made great things happen.

In truth, I am here to do the same in my own way. Yet I often sit and wait for the right moment or am immobilized by my insecurities and doubts.

My excuses are endless, but none are valid. This is not what You want from me.

Help me to sincerely commit to act. Bless my efforts so that I no longer fail You and others by what I have left undone.

Amen.

Day 356

Today's prayer: Lord . . .

Of all the gifts You have blessed me with, there is one that is totally mine and it cannot be added to.

It's my life! Thank You for it!

I cannot add to it, but I can certainly do things to detract from it!

Open my eyes to Your intent in giving it to me. Show me where I am squandering it and move me to doing those things, not the things that take me away from Your intent. My life is an amazing gift.

Thank You! I pray that I do not waste it!

Amen.

Day 357

Today's prayer: Lord . . .

The world is better for Your being here.

Thank You.

My life is better for my knowing You.

Thank You.

Help me to be the same in my part of this world so that this world is better for my being here. More important, ensure that others' lives are touched by my fleeting presence and that all of the thankfulness comes not to me but to You.

It is because of and through You that all glory and true success are made manifest. I commit to making it the reason I do what I do.

Amen.

Day 358

Today's prayer: Lord . . .

"We see in a mirror dimly."

This is so true. Our vision is filtered and biased by our feelings and intent.

You see us and the world clearly.

You see the past, present, and future and their purpose.

Help me to see myself and the world around me as it really is. As scary as this is, make me brave. Make me act.

Give me the clarity of vision that will narrow my journey and show me my purpose so that my walk may better serve You.

Amen.

Day 359

Today's prayer: Lord . . .

Your love for me shows in how patient You are with me.

I am far from what I should be, yet through Your love You focus my life on what is important and count every moment as a victory.

I commit to showing the world Your love through my patience and persistence. Help me to be an example of Your love so that others not only desire but also emulate.

Amen.

Day 360

Today's prayer: Lord . . .

You are love. When all things are taken away, only love remains.

Love is exhibited in kindness—kind words and kind acts.

Love only enters and exists in this world through what I do, what I say, how I do it, how I say it, and most important why I do it. The measure of my love is shown in those simple standards.

If I have not love, I am nothing. It is not the love given to me but the love I give that makes me who I am, and it is what will last.

I commit to kindness in thought, words, and deeds so that You are present in this world through us.

Why?

Because I love You.

Amen.

Day 361

Today's prayer: Lord . . .

You are love. We say that we know You, yet we often ask, "What is love?"

Love is not what is in our heart but what we do.

One way that we know love is that You show us love with Your patience. Love is patient.

You look to us in our time, not Yours.

You wait for us on our terms, not Yours.

True patience, like love, waits selflessly and demands nothing on its own schedule.

We commit to being more patient. In that simple act, real love is made manifest in this world, not in fleeting moments but constantly.

We wait on Your terms and Your timing. Why?

Because, like You, we are love.

Amen.

Day 362

Today's prayer: Lord . . .

You are living water. Just as water gives life, real love gives life.

As I think about water, I realize that good water comes from good wells and bad water from bad wells. It is all about the source and what is deep down that matters most.

I am a well of life and love in this world. Help me to look deep down and clean out what is deep inside, so that what comes from me is always good, true, and beautiful—and gives life to a dying world from You, my source, and for You, my reason for living.

Amen.

Day 363

Today's prayer: Lord . . .

It's time!

When You came into this world, You did it with purpose.

Why? Because it was time. The Father told You, and You wasted not a single opportunity in fulfilling what You were sent to do.

Thank You.

It is because You recognized that it was time. What You were, what You did, and what You continue to be make it possible for me to be and do what I can now according to Your call—when I recognize that it is time!

Thank You.

Drive me.

It's time.

Enter this world through me.

I am ready to follow Your perfect will rather than my imperfect, selfish desires.

It's time.

Amen.

Day 364

Today's prayer: Lord . . .

My past can be my greatest gift. It is filled with successes and failures. The value of my past is in direct proportion to how it has affected today's actions.

If the past repeats itself, it is my problem, not Yours, and the value of my past is diminished.

I realize the fact is that my refusal to learn from my past is in direct defiance of You.

If I learn, I act. If I don't learn, that is my choice and I repeat my failures.

There are messages in every situation. Today I commit to listening for myself and for others, always acting from the lessons You have lovingly sent.

Amen.

Day 365

Today's prayer: Lord . . .

If just one of these prayers touches the life of one person for but a moment . . .

And brings this person closer to You . . .

And helps them grow . . .

Or helps them see You more clearly . . .

Then this entire effort was worth it.

I long to hear, "Well done, good and faithful servant."

I will continue to strive, not for my glory but for Yours.

Amen.

Review Requested:

If you loved this book, would you please provide
a review at Amazon.com?

CPSIA information can be obtained
at www.ICGtesting.com
Printed in the USA
LVOW10s2141190217

524773LV00002B/125/P